EDEN END

A Play in Three Acts
BY
J. B. PRIESTLEY

SAMUEL FRENCH LIMITED
LONDON

Copyright © 1934 by J.B. Priestley
Copyright (Acting Edition) © 1935 by J.B. Priestley
All Rights Reserved

EDEN END is fully protected under the copyright laws of the British Commonwealth, including Canada, the United States of America, and all other countries of the Copyright Union. All rights, including professional and amateur stage productions, recitation, lecturing, public reading, motion picture, radio broadcasting, television and the rights of translation into foreign languages are strictly reserved.

ISBN 978-0-573-11650-6

www.samuelfrench.co.uk
www.samuelfrench.com

For Amateur Production Enquiries

United Kingdom and World
excluding north america

plays@samuelfrench.co.uk
020 7255 4302/01

Each title is subject to availability from Samuel French, depending upon country of performance.

CAUTION: Professional and amateur producers are hereby warned that *EDEN END* is subject to a licensing fee. Publication of this play does not imply availability for performance. Both amateurs and professionals considering a production are strongly advised to apply to the appropriate agent before starting rehearsals, advertising, or booking a theatre. A licensing fee must be paid whether the title is presented for charity or gain and whether or not admission is charged.

The Professional Rights in this play are controlled by United Agents LLP, 12-26 Lexington St, Soho, London W1F 0LE.

No one shall make any changes in this title for the purpose of production. No part of this book may be reproduced, stored in a retrieval system, or transmitted in any form, by any means, now known or yet to be invented, including mechanical, electronic, photocopying, recording, videotaping, or otherwise, without the prior written permission of the publisher. No one shall upload this title, or part of this title, to any social media websites.

The right of J.B. Priestley to be identified as author of this work has been asserted in accordance with Section 77 of the Copyright, Designs and Patents Act 1988.

EDEN END

Produced at the Duchess Theatre, London, on September 13th, 1934, with the following cast of characters:

WILFRED KIRBY	*John Teed.*
SARAH	*Nellie Bowman.*
LILIAN KIRBY	*Alison Leggatt.*
DR. KIRBY	*Edward Irwin.*
STELLA KIRBY	*Beatrix Lehmann.*
GEOFFREY FARRANT	*Franklyn Bellamy.*
CHARLES APPLEBY	*Ralph Richardson.*

The Play produced by IRENE HENTSCHEL.

SYNOPSIS OF SCENERY

The action takes place in the sitting-room of Dr. Kirby's house at Eden End, in the North of England, the last week in October, 1912.

ACT I.—Tuesday Afternoon.

ACT II.—Friday Afternoon.

ACT III.—SCENE 1.—Saturday Night.

SCENE 2.—Sunday Afternoon.

[To face page 7—"Eden End."]

[Photograph by Pollard Crowther.

EDEN END
ACT I

Scene.—*Sitting-room of* Dr. Kirby's *house, Eden End. A comfortable, well-worn room furnished in the taste of an earlier period. A door at the back, preferably up a few steps, leading from the rest of the house. A door on the* R. *leading to a small room, originally the nursery, now used by* Sarah *to sit in and do small jobs. A window at* L. *looking out upon a distant grey-green hill of the North-Country type. A bookcase on right wall. A telephone prominently placed in corner near door up* C. *Up stage on* L. *a cottage piano and old piano-stool.*
(*See Photograph of Scene.*)

Time.—*An afternoon of early autumn in the year* 1912.

Wilfred *is discovered at the piano, carefully picking out with one finger, and sometimes vamping an accompaniment with left hand, a waltz refrain from "Gipsy Love." He is wearing a tweed suit but a linen collar and dark tie. He is about twenty-four, and though sunburned and in possession of a small moustache, he looks young, unsophisticated. After a few moments, during which he can improve a little and even attempt to sing the tune,* Sarah *enters through door on* R., *carrying some things she has presumably been ironing in her little room.* Sarah *is an old North-Country nurse, now about seventy, a queer old creature, at once simple and shrewd, and very earthy. She still slaves for all the family, but her tone towards them is still indulgent, as if they were children.*

Wilfred. I'm getting it, Sarah. I'm getting it.
Sarah (*going to above table* L.C.). You've been at it long enough. (*She puts a pile of shirts on the table.*)
Wilfred. Now just listen. (*He plays again. Wheeling round.*) What do you think of that?
Sarah. It sounds like proper playing—a'most.
Wilfred. Not so much of the *almost*. What more do you want?
Sarah. Well, I'm not saying you're not doing very well with it. But you'll never shape at it like Miss Stella, never in all your born days you won't.
Wilfred. Do you know how many times you've said that?
Sarah. For playing and singing and such-like——

WILFRED. She was wonderful. I know. (*He turns back to piano and plays some chords.*) Well, I'm wonderful too.

SARAH (*going up to him and dusting his shoulder*). You're a right untidy lad.

WILFRED. I'm not a lad.

SARAH (*coming back to above table*). Bother I've had wi' your clothes.

WILFRED (*turning to her*). Did you do anything to my blue shirt?

SARAH. Ay, that's mended. And two more beside. And two of the doctor's.

WILFRED. When I'm in Africa, Sarah, black women wash my clothes.

SARAH. I remember seeing four black women once at Martinbro Fair. Black as your boots they were. And fuzzy hair.

WILFRED. Where I work, when I go away, there are thousands and thousands of people like that. And I'm the boss. And then when I come home on leave, you call me a lad.

SARAH. These women kept rubbing their teeth with bits of stick, I remember. And I fancy it was the same year you went and fell into that duck-pond just outside Martinbro. You wor only a little lad and you had your best sailor suit on. (*She goes to door up* C., *taking clothes with her.*)

WILFRED. What would you do if you saw a hippopotamus?

SARAH. I don't know what they are. I've no time to be bothering wi' such little things now.

(*She goes out and closes the door.*)

WILFRED (*making a complete revolution on piano-stool*). Good old Sarah!

SARAH (*reopening door*). You get on wi' your piano playing, and frame a bit better.

(*She closes door.*)

(WILFRED *begins playing again, then leaves off, as if in disgust with himself.*)

(*Off.*) What about Gregson's, Miss Lilian?

LILIAN (*off*). All right, I'll look after that.

(*Hearing the voices off stage,* WILFRED *hastily plunges into a very noisy, inaccurate rendering of the waltz.*)

(LILIAN KIRBY *enters. She is a year or two older than her brother; neither pretty nor ugly; neatly but not well dressed in indoor clothes. She has more sweetness of character than would superficially appear from what she says and does. When she is not taking refuge in sarcasm, she is quick and eager.*)

LILIAN (*going to chair below fire*). What's that awful row? (*She picks up book, which is lying open on chair.*)

WILFRED (*shouting above his playing*). That's the waltz from "Gipsy Love."
LILIAN (*sitting on pouf to read her book*). It sounds a mess.
WILFRED (*finishing his playing and turning to her*). That's because I can't play it properly.
LILIAN. That's obvious.
WILFRED. You ought to hear it as they do it. Gertie Millar and Robert Michaelis.
LILIAN (*ironically*). Wonderful!
WILFRED (*ignoring this, eagerly*). You know—somehow—it completely carried me away. It's rot, I suppose—
LILIAN (*now trying to read*). Of course it's rot.
WILFRED. Yes, but just think. (*He breaks off.*) You *might* listen, Lilian. Hang it all, I'm not always here to tell you things. And I listen to you.
LILIAN (*looking up from book*). Go on then.
WILFRED (*warming as he goes on*). Just think of it. Back from Africa. London. First night on leave. A jolly good dinner with two other chaps from the Company. Then Daly's. (*He rises and goes above table to* R. *of it.*) Lights, and everybody in the stalls dressed, stunning girls, the band playing—and then Gertie Millar —and oh—everything. Do you know, Lilian, I felt quite queer. I nearly cried.
LILIAN. Did you?
WILFRED. I didn't really cry, you know. But I nearly did. Felt like it.
LILIAN. That's the only bit you haven't told me twenty times already.
WILFRED (*hotly*). That's not true.
LILIAN. Sorry, but it is.

(WILFRED *goes to piano and looks through pile of music on it.*)

I can tell you the names of the chaps—as you call them—who went with you that night. One was called Patterson, and he comes from Cumberland and he's a good footballer. The other's called Bell —Bell—Bellingham——
WILFRED (*gloomily over his left shoulder*). Bellington.
LILIAN. That's it. Not much difference. He's called Bellington and he comes from Devonshire, and he's got a sister who's married to a Captain in the Navy. There!
WILFRED (*huffily, going to window*). Sorry. Didn't know I'd been boring you.
LILIAN (*beginning to read*). You haven't. Don't apologize.

(*She looks at him as he stands looking out of the window. He starts to whistle.*)

By the way, you wouldn't like to walk into the village to give an order to Gregson's, would you?

WILFRED. No, thanks. (*He whistles a little of the waltz.*)
LILIAN. Then I suppose I'll have to go. Soon. (*She begins reading again.*)
WILFRED (*turning to look at her*). Don't you ever get tired of reading?
LILIAN (*without looking up*). Yes.
WILFRED. You're always reading.
LILIAN (*without looking up*). I'm not.
    (WILFRED *crosses above table to her.*)
I spend most of the day looking after this house, and Dad, and you when you're at home.
WILFRED. Yes, but the minute you've done you begin reading. (*Leaning over her, from above her, to see the title—his head close to hers.*) What's that?
LILIAN. Wells's new book. "Marriage." (*She goes on reading.*)
WILFRED (*going to club fender*). You never seem to stop reading H. G. Wells. I don't know how you can stick him. I can't. Doesn't seem to like anything. He always makes me feel so uncomfortable. What's the point of reading if it makes you feel uncomfortable? It's bad enough in real life. (*He takes out packet of cigarettes.*)
LILIAN (*still reading*). That's stupid.
WILFRED. Why is it stupid?
    (*She gives no reply but goes on reading.*)
Geoffrey Farrant was saying just the same thing the other day.
    (*She looks up. He guffaws.*)
LILIAN (*crossly*). Don't be absurd. (*She hesitates.*) Did Geoffrey really say that?
WILFRED (*teasing*). Wouldn't you like to know?
LILIAN. It doesn't matter in the least.
WILFRED. Is Geoffrey coming round to-night?
LILIAN. I don't know. He might.
WILFRED (*after lighting a cigarette*). Good old Geoffrey! By Jove, when I was a kid, about fourteen, I used to think he was marvellous.
LILIAN. Yes, I know.
WILFRED. That was when he was mad on Stella. He was my hero all right; regular soldier, captain, wounded in the Boer War— I used to follow him round like a little dog. I must have been a nuisance when he wanted to be alone with Stella. (*Crossing to table.*) She used to tease him and say he came round just to be a hero to me. That's a long time ago. Nearly ten years. (*He sits on edge of table.*) I say.
LILIAN (*rather wearily*). Well?
WILFRED. You see a lot of Geoffrey these days. Does he ever **talk** about Stella?

LILIAN (*shortly*). No, why should he? Give me a cigarette.
WILFRED. What for? You don't smoke.
LILIAN. I do if I want to. Give me one, please. (*She holds out her hand.*)
WILFRED (*rising and going to her*). Oh, all right, Christabel Pankhurst. (*Giving her one.*) But mind you don't make yourself sick.
LILIAN. Why should I? I'm better at not being sick than you are.

(WILFRED *goes back to table.*)

You admit yourself you're always sea-sick.
WILFRED. That's different. Besides, just you try going through the Bay of Biscay in winter—as I've done, three times now.
LILIAN (*rising and going to mantelpiece for matches*). And then there was the time when we both went on the swings at Martinbro Fair, and you were horribly sick and I wasn't. (*She awkwardly lights cigarette, and then, when it gets going, takes too deep a breath and coughs.*)
WILFRED. You see. Take it easy. What if Dad marches in?
LILIAN. He won't mind. Mother would have minded, but Dad won't. (*She sits in chair above fireplace. She does not make a success of her smoking.*)
WILFRED. One of our chaps in Nigeria told me his father wouldn't let him do *anything*. Terribly strict. That's why he cleared out.
LILIAN. Lucky chap.
WILFRED (*wandering up to the telephone*). You know, when I came home and saw the telephone, brand new, I thought I'd be able to have a lot of fun with it, but I haven't. There's nobody to ring up here in Eden End.
LILIAN. Who were you ringing up yesterday?
WILFRED (*indignantly*). You were listening!
LILIAN. I wasn't. I happened to hear your voice when I was in the hall, putting some things away. Who was it?
WILFRED (*turning away*). Oh—just somebody I know.
LILIAN. A girl, obviously. You're keeping her very dark, aren't you?
WILFRED. I don't know her very well, and, anyhow, she lives miles away, the other side of Martinbro. (*Going towards window.*) Never mind about her.
LILIAN. I'm not minding. But I suspect she's a barmaid and that's why you can get her on the telephone.
WILFRED. You know, Lilian, one thing puzzles me.
LILIAN. And if she's a barmaid, on the telephone, and the other side of Martinbro——-

(WILFRED *crosses above table to her.*)

—she's probably at that big pub at the cross-roads near Denly Dene—the " White Hart."

WILFRED (*angrily*). Will you listen?
LILIAN. Do you really like her, Wilfred? Or do you just think that being sweet on a barmaid is very manly and West African?
WILFRED. I'm trying to say something important.
LILIAN. Well, what is it?
WILFRED. You don't really want to know. You'll only laugh.
LILIAN. You've got to risk that. I mightn't. Tell me.
WILFRED (*crossing to fireplace and leaning against mantel, his back to her, hesitating*). It's difficult to explain. But I feel as if I'm being done in the eye.
LILIAN. You probably are.
WILFRED. You see, when I'm out there, in Africa, I think of Eden End here—home and you and Dad, and everything, and I long for leave, and when at last it comes—(*turning to her*) well, of course, it's ripping. But then when I've been here a week or two——
LILIAN. It all begins to look dull. Doesn't it?
WILFRED. Well, not quite as bad as that. (*He crosses towards table.*)
LILIAN. Yes it is. Don't sound so apologetic. I don't blame you.
WILFRED (*drifting below table and up* L. *of it*). Anyhow, it isn't what I expected. And then I begin to think about Nigeria, and I begin to feel it won't be bad getting back there. But now I know that once I *am* back there I'll be longing to be on leave again, and this place will seem all different. I've got into a sort of life where I'm never in the right place at the right time. (*He sits on chair* L. *of table.*)
LILIAN. Poor Wilfred. You were just like that when you were at school.
WILFRED. I know. And I thought it would be different when I left school and grew up. Perhaps it will, later on.
LILIAN. Perhaps it will. You've plenty of time.
WILFRED (*building castles with playing cards on table*). Things can't stay like this. When I've more money I shall have more fun on leave. And it'll be more amusing out there when I'm promoted. It's Nineteen Twelve now. In three or four years time—say in Nineteen Sixteen—I may have a district of my own.
LILIAN. Could I come out and see you then?
WILFRED. You might. Depends where I'm sent.
LILIAN. You may be married before then.
WILFRED. I don't suppose so. Three or four years isn't really a long time. Hurry up, Nineteen Sixteen. Sounds a nice ripe sort of year, doesn't it?—Nineteen Sixteen. (*He knocks down his castle.*)

(*From the door come three deliberate knocks. The two look at it sharply, rather startled—though they must avoid any nervous jump.* WILFRED *goes to the door and opens it.* SARAH *enters, carrying a large basket heaped with old clothes.*)

SARAH (*putting basket on table, breathlessly*). I didn't want to put this down to open the door because I'm not so good at stooping as I was——

(WILFRED *drifts back to* L. *of table and sits.*)

—gives me palpitations—and I've been stooping enough.

LILIAN. What have you been doing?

SARAH. I've been up in the back garret, samming up these old clothes for the doctor. He wants to give 'em away. Eh, and look what I found. (*She holds out an old fancy costume.*)

LILIAN. What is it?

SARAH. Don't you remember? It's very same dress Miss Stella wore that time she acted in the Town Hall at Martinbro, and they all clapped her so long, and she came back and told her poor mother she was going on the stage for a living, and we had such a do—all shouting and bawling and crying. Don't you remember it?

WILFRED. I do.

LILIAN. Yes, I do now. (*She rises, puts her cigarette out and goes to* R. *of* SARAH.)

SARAH. And I should think so. I helped her to make it, and right bonny she looked in it. But she never took it with her when she went, and it's been behind some boxes in the back garret. I fancy your mother threw it there. Moths has been at it a bit, but I'm thinking it 'ud clean and mend.

LILIAN. What for? It's quite useless.

SARAH. How do you know? We might send it to her and she might be glad of it for her acting.

WILFRED (*laughing*). You're cracked, Sarah.

SARAH (*indignant*). What's there to laugh at, I'd like to know?

LILIAN. Nothing. Only, you see, we couldn't send it to Stella —even if it would be useful—because we don't know where she is.

SARAH. Isn't she out—you know—where's it? That big place?

WILFRED. Timbuctoo.

SARAH. Not Timbuctoo neither, you daft lad. It's where she said there was all eucalyptus.

LILIAN. It was Australia. But that was three years ago, and we haven't heard anything from her since.

SARAH. Is it three year since we heard last?

LILIAN. Yes. And she's been away more than eight years.

SARAH (*her face working as she fingers the costume*). I didn't think it was so long. I'm getting old and I forget. I'm dreaming half my time.

LILIAN (*looking at the costume and holding it against herself*). I remember. It was pretty. I believe I was jealous because I hadn't one like it.

SARAH. Yes, you wor. You wor a jealous little madam in them days, let me tell you. See. I sewed them on myself for her. It was all a secret. She used to sneak in there (*pointing to door* R.) to try it on. It only seems yesterday. I mun sort these out.

(LILIAN *puts costume back on basket.*)

WILFRED. Here, I'll take them.

(*He goes below table and picks up basket, etc., and takes them into room* R.)

SARAH. Your father's in. He called at Gregson's.

(*She starts to move towards door* R. *The telephone bell rings. She turns and looks at it mistrustfully.*)

That wants answering now. Daft thing. Got to wait on a machine, that's what we're coming to. It'll never get me waiting on it, and it can ring its head off.

(*She goes into room* R. LILIAN *goes to the telephone, but* DR. KIRBY *enters* C. *quickly and forestalls her. He is a pleasant, homely man about sixty, wearing an old house-coat over a dark professional suit. He attends to the telephone rather pompously and proudly.* LILIAN *sits below fireplace, taking socks from work-basket on bookcase and darning.*)

DR. KIRBY (L. *of telephone*). Hello, yes. Yes, Dr. Kirby here. Oh—is that you, William ? . . . She's what ? . . . Oh I see . . . Well, what do you expect ? . . . No pains ? . . . I see . . . Yes, keep her warm. And don't worry. Nothing new. It's all happened before. . . . That's right, let me know. And, William, just keep out of the Eden Moor Hotel for a night or two, will you ? . . . That's it. You're not in the right state of mind to do yourself any good in the bar of the Eden Moor . . . (*Chuckles.*) All right. Don't worry. (*He puts down receiver and rings off, then wanders to above table*—R. *of it.*) William Sugden worrying about his wife. She'll be all right. Stronger than he is. Now it just shows you, Lilian, how useful a telephone is here. That little chat across the wires has saved William or me a useless journey. Pity we hadn't it here years ago. We're too old-fashioned round here. Out of date.

LILIAN. You don't think you're out of date, do you ?

DR. KIRBY. Me ? Years out of date. I've just been trying to understand what some of these young fellows are writing now in the medical journals. Too clever for me. Too Nineteen Twelve altogether. But I could probably give 'em points when it comes to dealing with William Sugden and his wife.

(WILFRED *enters from room* R.)

Hello, Wilfred, what have you been doing in there ?

(*The light begins to fade.*)

WILFRED (*going up to* R. *of him*). Helping Sarah to sort out some old clothes for you.

DR. KIRBY. Good. They can do with some of them down in

Act I.]   EDEN END.   15

the village. Lloyd George is going to give 'em ninepence for fourpence soon, with me thrown in, but in the meantime we'll give them some old clothes to be going on with. (*He goes up towards door* C.)
WILFRED (*crossing below table to window-seat*). Would you like to hear my gramophone, Dad?
DR. KIRBY. No, thank you. I've got to get back to the surgery. But if I was staying I'd just as soon not hear your gramophone. I've got to listen to too many patients to want to hear mechanical music—if it is music. By the way, old Burton tells me they had a fire in the post office at Martinbro late last night. He said they think it's suffragettes. Lot of nonsense. They've got suffragettes on the brain, some of 'em. (*He gets to door* C.)
WILFRED. Well, it might be, Dad.
DR. KIRBY (*turning at door*). What, at Martinbro! What would they be doing there? Looking for Mr. Asquith! All nonsense. (*At first step.*) And talking about nonsense, I forgot to tell you I've just been invited to dine at Grosvenor House with the Duke of Westminster.
LILIAN
WILFRED } (*together*). Dad, you haven't?
DR. KIRBY. I have. And so has everybody else—on one condition—that we each pay a thousand pounds to Chamberlain's birthday fund for Tariff Reform. I'm not accepting.

(*He goes out. Pause.*)

WILFRED (*wandering to piano, restlessly*). We ought to have a billiard table here. (*He gets to above the table.*) If I got more chance to play, I believe I should be good at billiards. (*Crossing towards* LILIAN.) I made a break of twenty-seven when I played at the club at Akassa.
LILIAN (*staring at him, quietly*). Isn't it ridiculous that you should go to all these places while I have to stay here?
WILFRED. No, I don't see that.
LILIAN. But I used to be much more adventurous than you, and much keener on exploring and wild places. I'll bet I've read far more about Africa than you have.
WILFRED. What's that? Reading about it! (*Going back to above table.*) I've been.
LILIAN. Do you know what I'd rather have done than anything else in the world? I'd rather have gone with Captain Scott to the South Pole. And if he lectures about it when he comes back I shall go, I don't care where it is.
WILFRED (*at piano*). Well, you can't be so jolly adventurous—as you call it—else you'd have cleared out. After all, Stella did.
LILIAN (*rather bitterly*). Yes, Stella did. And what happened then? Mother died. I had to come home and look after the house and Father. It's easy enough to do what Stella did—just to clear out and do what you want to do.

WILFRED (*wandering to window*). Yes, but she knew what she wanted to do.

LILIAN. Perhaps I did, too.

WILFRED (*turning and kneeling on chair* L. *of table*). You know, that night I went to Daly's, I thought how queer it would be if I suddenly saw Stella come on the stage.

LILIAN (*with slight sardonic emphasis*). Very queer. (*She rises and crosses to* R. *of table with darning to get nearer light from window.*)

WILFRED. I always look at advertisements and programmes and bills to see if she's on. It's silly having a sister on the stage if you've never *seen* her on the stage. Wouldn't it be grand if she became a star like Gertie Millar or Phyllis Dare?

LILIAN (*sardonically*). Yes. And if the British West African Company suddenly appointed you managing director. And if the King fell ill and they all said, " Send for Dr. Kirby of Eden End." And if Pierpoint Morgan or Rockefeller said, " I must give Lilian Kirby a million pounds, she's been such a good girl." (*She sits* R. *of table.*)

WILFRED (*guffawing*). And if old Sarah won a prize for doing the Turkey Trot. And if Geoffrey Farrant—what do we do for Geoffrey?

LILIAN. Something with horses or dogs in it.

WILFRED. We'll let him win next year's Derby then. You're not very keen on horses and dogs, are you?

LILIAN (*coldly*). What's that got to do with it?

WILFRED (*grinning*). Nothing.

LILIAN. Don't be an oaf.

WILFRED. One of our chaps in Benin used to own two racehorses when he was in England. Awful nut. (*Going to above gramophone on window-seat.*) What about a good old row on the gramophone?

LILIAN. Must you?

WILFRED. Yes, I must. (*He starts gramophone record* " Everybody's doing it " *and listens to introduction.*) I shall take this back with me. (*He listens to some more.*) You know, these things are getting awfully good.

LILIAN. I say, can your gramophone see?

WILFRED. Not very well.

LILIAN. Neither can my darning!—Let's light the lamps.

(WILFRED *lights piano lamp at same time as* LILIAN *lights standard lamp below fire. He meets her* C. *and dances her round until they hear a noise off.* WILFRED *crosses hurriedly below table to stop gramophone. They hear a voice coming through the door. The voice,* STELLA'S, *must be audible everywhere, but it does not matter if actual words are not caught. Actually she is saying,* " Yes, put it down there, please. What do I pay you? There you are. Thank you." STELLA *is five or six years older than* LILIAN, *and looks her age, but is extremely attractive. She is dressed as an* actress, hoping to be smart, would be, dressed at that time, but her clothes must not be really good or very new, so that it is obvious to an acute feminine spectator that she is not really flourishing. She plays at once in a higher key than the rest of the family, and is obviously an actress as well as a prodigal daughter. All her emotions are quite sincere, but she cannot help being a little larger than life. This gradually wears off during her stay until the scene of her departure, when there are glimpses of the actress again.

She enters C., looks at WILFRED, who is above table, then at LILIAN, who is by the fire, then back to WILFRED. She gives him her muff.)

WILFRED. Stella!
STELLA. Oh, it's Wilfred! All grown up. And a moustache. (*Embraces and kisses him. Then looks at* LILIAN.) And Lilian. (*Crossing over to her and kissing her.*) All grown up, too. Here, let me take this damned hat off. (*Hastily takes it off and puts hat and bag on table.*) Lilian darling, you're not at all what I expected you to look like, and yet you're completely Lilian and just right. Isn't it odd? (*Looking round.*) And everything just the same. Only smaller.

(SARAH *comes in from* R. *and stands just inside door, staring at* STELLA *with puckered face.*)

(*Seeing her, dropping her stole on floor and rushing over.*) Why, Sarah! My precious, precious lovely old Sarah! (*Kisses her.*)

(LILIAN *picks up stole and goes up* C. ; WILFRED *puts muff on window-seat.*)

SARAH (*in tears*). Nay—I can't talk.
STELLA (*laughing and crying*). And I can't.
SARAH (*making an effort*). Eh—you haven't altered a bit, love.
STELLA. Oh, but I have. I'm old, Sarah—yes, old. I'll never see thirty again. My hair's turning grey.
SARAH. It isn't.
STELLA. Some of it is. I pulled three grey hairs out yesterday. (*Going to* R. *of* LILIAN—*up* C.) Where's Dad? Is he—all right?
LILIAN. Yes. He's in the surgery.
WILFRED (L. *of table*). Shall I tell him?
STELLA. No, don't disturb him. We'll give him a surprise. Is he just the same?
WILFRED. Of course.
STELLA. *Of course?* (*She crosses below* LILIAN *to* R. *of table.*) There isn't any *of course* about it. Oh, Wilfred—that just shows how young you are, in spite of that moustache. People change. Everything changes. Does he still watch birds and collect eighteenth-century engravings?
LILIAN. Yes. Dad hasn't changed at all.
STELLA. Thank God!

(STELLA *sits on* R. *edge of table.* WILFRED *sits on chair* L. *of table.*
LILIAN *comes to* R. *of* STELLA. SARAH *goes to above and between* LILIAN *and* STELLA.)

LILIAN. But why didn't you tell us you were coming?

STELLA. Oh—my dear—I couldn't. I didn't know. (*She puts an arm round* SARAH.) And I couldn't just write. I think I was afraid to. Either I had to stay away or come just like this, with a rush. Don't you understand?

LILIAN. Yes. You'd been away so long.

STELLA. So long. And to so many places.

WILFRED. Where have you been, Stella?

STELLA. Where haven't I been? All over England. Then out East. Then Australia—I wrote to you from there——

SARAH. Yes, you did, love.

STELLA. I was nearly dying of homesickness when I wrote that letter. You can't imagine what it's like.

WILFRED (*proudly*). I can. I'm in Nigeria now. Got a job with the British West African Development Company. I'm on leave.

STELLA (*smiling at him*). Africa and on leave. Wilfred, it's incredible. It seems only yesterday since you were a fat little schoolboy. I'm sorry, but it does. I didn't really believe in that moustache. (*Touching it with her finger.*) Somehow I thought of you just sticking it on for fun.

WILFRED. I'm twenty-four. I've been four years with the British West African.

STELLA. Isn't that wonderful? And then after Australia, I went to America. We travelled thousands of miles. I seem to have lived in railway trains—with cinders in my eye and a headache—for centuries. None of it real. Like a long stupid dream. And now I'm home. You don't know what it means.

SARAH. Aren't you famished, love? Can't I get you something?

STELLA. No, thank you. Not just now, Sarah. (*She rises and looks about her, then comes down to* R.C.—*back to audience.*)

(LILIAN *pushes chair under* R. *of table.*)

It's just as I remembered it, only so much smaller. All the time I've been away, it's been shrinking and shrinking. Like life. Oh—(*darting over to fireplace*) there's the china castle.

(LILIAN *goes to* C., WILFRED *moves below table to* L. *of* LILIAN, *while* SARAH *is above table*—R. *of it—giving the effect of a group, following* STELLA *about the room.*)

Still there. (*Picking it up.*) Not broken. All sorts of things can get broken—people can be broken—and yet a thing like this can go on and on. (*Holding it, looking at it.*) I remember how I used to wonder what was happening inside it. Tiny people all made of china.

Act I.]   EDEN END.   19

(*The group comes nearer to* STELLA.)

WILFRED. You used to tell me stories about that castle.

STELLA. And look (*putting the castle back on mantelpiece and picking up goat*)—the boy's still riding on his goat. What did we used to call him?

LILIAN. Llewellyn. Because he came from Wales.

STELLA. Yes. Dear, dear Llewellyn. His nice silly face has come popping up in dreams. I saw him distinctly once—oh, when was it?—on some long, awful train journey, hot and dusty. And there was Llewellyn riding his goat. (*She gives the goat to* LILIAN *and crosses below her to above piano*.) And here's Coblentz. (*Looking at old colour print* L. *of door*.)

(WILFRED *goes to* R. *of* STELLA *and* SARAH *moves to below piano.* LILIAN *puts goat back on mantel*.)

The three soldiers talking. The man carrying the load. The woman with the red petticoat. And the two holding hands. Do you remember how we used to look at it for hours and wonder what was happening round the corner? But where's the other one, you know, Frankfort, with the river and the barges and the little fat woman?

WILFRED. Yes, where is Frankfort? I hadn't noticed it was gone.

SARAH. That's the picture that fell down, isn't it?

LILIAN. Yes, it was broken. About a year ago.

(*Pause*.)

(STELLA *sits* L. *of table,* WILFRED *sits upstage edge of table,* SARAH *drops down* L. *and* LILIAN *stands behind chair* R. *of table*.)

STELLA. Tell me about people. The Mowbrays and the Oldroyds and the Burtons—and everybody. Oh—and my old admirer, Geoffrey Farrant. What's happened to him?

LILIAN. He's still here. His father died.

STELLA. Is he married? Do you ever see him?

LILIAN. He's not married.

WILFRED. And we often see him. He's a great pal of Lilian's now.

LILIAN. Where are your things?

STELLA. My trunk? It's in the hall. I got a trap from the station, but I didn't know the man who brought me. I didn't recognize anybody at the station either. But Eden Moor and Eden End looked just the same. And, coming up, there was a lovely deep rich autumn smell—smoke and dead leaves and the moors all mixed up—and I was absolutely drowned in it and I didn't seem to have been away at all. Millions of smells, mostly beastly, that I've smelt these last eight or nine years were completely washed out. Nothing had really happened. I might have

B

only been in to Martinbro for the day. You were still at school, Wilfred. You'd only just left, Lilian, and you'd still two long plaits. And Dad and Mother—— (*She breaks off, hesitates, then in a low voice.*) Was it awful, Lilian about Mother?

LILIAN (*quietly*). Yes, for a time. But it's six years ago, you know. She wasn't ill very long, but she'd a lot of pain. It was Dad I was sorry for.

(STELLA *begins to cry quietly.*)

SARAH (*putting a hand on her shoulder*). Miss Stella—love.

STELLA (*rising and crossing below* LILIAN *to fireplace—through her tears*). Such a silly thing happened in the train. A man sitting opposite me—he looked like Winston Churchill, only fatter—carefully unpacked a lot of sandwiches on the seat, stood up for something, and then suddenly sat down on the sandwiches.

(STELLA *sits on club fender,* LILIAN *sits above fire, while* SARAH *crosses and sits below fire.*)

There was another woman in the carriage, and we suddenly laughed and laughed, and then the man laughed too. They were very eggy sandwiches. Why are some things so silly?

WILFRED (*rising and crossing to fire*). Do you remember the time when a little man with a very funny face—(*sitting on hearthrug above pouf*) what was his name?—Flockton——

(*They all laugh.*)

—and we started giggling and then had to go outside in turns to laugh?

STELLA. Yes, Mr. Flockton. And it was much worse for me because I was so much older and I had to be polite. And then the time when poor Aunt Mary brought that new bun flour?

(*They all laugh again.*)

WILFRED. Yes, and the time when the young man called Egg-something came to see you and dropped the tea-tray?

LILIAN. And the time when we all went to the Mowbrays for a party on the wrong day?

(*Again they all laugh.*)

STELLA. And the snow was so thick we had to stay, and they were so cross, and we were so cross, and all the chimneys smoked.

(*There is now a big laugh.*)

WILFRED (*laughing*). And I broke a huge ornament and put the pieces in the coal scuttle.

(WILFRED *rolls on his back with laughter. The others laugh long and heartily, ending in sighs for breath.*)

STELLA. I was thinking about all those things coming up in the train. And I've got millions of questions to ask.
WILFRED. So have we, haven't we, Lilian?
LILIAN. I suppose you'd like your old room, wouldn't you?
STELLA. I'd love it if it's free.
LILIAN. It's full of odds and ends at the moment——
SARAH (*eagerly*). I'll get it ready, Miss Lilian.
LILIAN (*rising and going to door* C.). No, I'll do it. Wilfred can give me a hand. There may be some furniture to move.
WILFRED. Rather. (*He gets up.*)
STELLA. Can't I do anything?
LILIAN. No. You're tired. Besides, you don't know where things are now. And Dad will be in in a minute. You wait here.

(*She goes out at door up* C.)

WILFRED (L. *of armchair above fire*). You know, Stella, when you were home I was only a kid and didn't bother about the theatre, but now I'm very keen. I saw " Gipsy ove " at Daly's a few weeks ago—and you've got to tell me all about it.
STELLA. All right. I'll tell you miles and miles of it. (*She rises and kneels in armchair above fire, beside him.*)

(SARAH *goes into room* R.)

WILFRED. Good. I expect you've done jolly well, haven't you? I was telling Lilian only this afternoon how I always looked out for your name, but never saw it.
STELLA. I've been out of England so much, you see.
WILFRED. Yes, that accounts for it. Well, you're looking an awful swell.
STELLA. I should have thought I was looking like nothing on earth.
WILFRED. I expect you've had a marvellous time, haven't you?
STELLA. Well—mixed, you know.
WILFRED (*moving away towards table*). You'll find it pretty dull here.
STELLA. I shan't. (*Draws a long breath.*) It's heavenly. Even though you have been in Africa and come on leave you can't imagine what it means to me to be back again—home. It's real. Everything's real again.
WILFRED. I'm going to give Lilian a hand with your room. Then I'll come down and ask you thousands of questions. (*He goes to door up* C., *then hesitates.*) I say, you don't think this moustache looks silly, do you?
STELLA (*crossing to* R. *of him, hands on his shoulders*). Wilfred, it's a *grand* moustache, and you look a real African adventurer with it. It's tremendously exciting to be a sister to such a moustache. In a year or two it's going to be a terrific heart-breaker.

WILFRED (*smiling*). You're pulling my leg. You always did, you know.

STELLA. Well, isn't it nice that I'm starting all over again ?

(SARAH *re-enters from* R., *carrying dress behind her back.*)

WILFRED (*shyly*). Yes. (*Smiles.*) Good old Stella !

(*He goes out up* C.)

(STELLA *looks after him and smiles. Then she turns and sees* SARAH.)

STELLA (*going to above table*). I think Wilfred's grown up to be a very nice young man. (*She takes mirror from handbag to straighten her hair.*) Don't you ?

(SARAH *goes to* C.)

SARAH. Oh—Master Wilfred's all right. But he's only a bit of a lad, for all his big talk. Miss Lilian's different. She's properly grown up. Always was a bit old-fashioned. Never gave herself away. And there's times now when—dang me !—you'd think she wor fifty—to hear her talk. Not that she talks much.

STELLA. I don't suppose poor Lilian's had a very easy life all these years I've been away. She's—— (*Grappling for the right expression.*) Sort of sunk into herself. On her guard, somehow. Almost as if I were a stranger. Perhaps I am a stranger, Sarah. But I don't seem like one to myself—only Stella Kirby, back home again in Eden End. (*She goes to window.*)

SARAH. And look what I found—(*coming to below and* R. *of table*) not an hour since—it might ha' been waiting for you to come home. Look. (*Holds out fancy costume.*)

STELLA (*getting to below table*). Why, it's the one I wore, ages ago, in that show at the Town Hall at Martinbro. (*Taking the costume.*) The one you and I made, Sarah.

SARAH. I know it is. I was going to clean and mend it. Moths has been at it.

STELLA. The moths have been at us all, Sarah darling. But I never thought I'd see this costume again. The excitement there was here about it ! Do you remember ?

SARAH. I should think I do.

STELLA. I thought I was a real actress the night I put this on.

SARAH. Well, they clapped you enough.

STELLA. More than some people have clapped me since. That was the night. Look at it. Pathetic !

SARAH. Why, I see nowt wrong wi' it, except where moths has been. It's a right bonny dress. I thowt so then and I think so now.

STELLA. So do I. It's a lovely dress. (*Holding it against herself and crossing below table to fire.*) The belle and leading juvenile of the Martinbro Amateur Dramatic Society. And fat old Mr. Burton gave me a box of chocolates, do you remember?

SARAH. Ay, and he'd have given a lot more besides chocolates if you'd let him, that chap would.

(STELLA *sits on pouf*.)

I've heard tales of him since. (*Crossing to* L. *of* STELLA.) Eh, I'm thankful to have seen this day, love. I've prayed to be spared to see you come home.

STELLA. I'm sorry I have been so long.

SARAH. You didn't forget me?

STELLA. Never, never, never. All over the world, in the oddest places, I've thought about you, longed to see you again. You needn't pray any more. I've come home.

SARAH (*looking hard at her*). You've always been a bonny piece. You wor a grand baby, and a fine little lass, and a bonny young woman when you grew up. (*She holds* STELLA'S *chin*.)

STELLA. Bless you for those kind words.

SARAH. But there's lines in that face that weren't there when I last saw it.

STELLA. I'm getting on. And all those years I was away haven't been easy.

SARAH. No, that's it. I can see as much. You've had your troubles, haven't you?

(STELLA *does not reply*.)

(*Crossing above her and sitting in chair below fire*.) Nay, you can tell me even if you never tell another soul. I'll say nowt.

STELLA. Yes. I've had my troubles.

SARAH. Disappointments?

STELLA. Yes. A fair share.

SARAH (*gently*). Didn't they treat you well on the stage, love?

STELLA. Nearly as well as I deserved, I suppose. But—and this is our secret, Sarah I wasn't the great actress I thought I was going to be. I wasn't bad. I'm not bad. But somehow I've never been able to do what I thought I could do. Something gets in the way. I feel it all inside, but it doesn't come out right. I've disappointed myself. I think even Mother would have been sorry for me if she'd known. I don't say I've had wonderful chances, but I have had chances. And somehow I've missed them. Perhaps I came nearer to being a really good actress the night I wore this pathetic thing than I've ever done since. It's all gone wrong, Sarah, my dear. My work, my life. Oh—I'm a dismal failure. (*She breaks down*.)

SARAH (*rising and going above* STELLA, *hands on her shoulders*). Don't worry, love, don't worry. There's plenty of time. You're young.

STELLA. No, I'm not.

Dr. KIRBY (*off* C.). You must ask Miss Lilian.
SARAH. I think I hear the doctor.
STELLA (*springing up, alarmed*). Dad mustn't see me like this.
(SARAH *takes the dress from her.* STELLA *crosses hastily below* SARAH *to table for handbag and returns to fire, doing her face.*)
And he mustn't know.
SARAH. He won't from me. Nobody will. I'll see if he's there.
(*She goes to door up* C. *and goes out.* STELLA *hastily concludes her powdering and begins to look brighter.*)
(DR. KIRBY *comes in* C. *and stands amazed.*)
DR. KIRBY. Is it Stella?
STELLA. Yes, Father.
(*With a little cry, she runs over to him, and he meets her at the bottom of the steps and they kiss and hug one another.* STELLA *ends up on* DR. KIRBY'S L.)
You're just the same, Dad. Only a little greyer, that's all.
DR. KIRBY. No, I'm a lot older. And you're older too, you know. I'm not going to flatter you even if you are a famous actress. (*He takes her right arm and walks her across to fire.*) You look a bit tired. But then I expect you are after your journey. Where did you come from?
STELLA. London. I caught the eleven-o'clock to Martinbro.
DR. KIRBY. Ah, yes—the good old eleven-o'clock. Why didn't you let us know? We'd have had the fatted calf ready for you. (*He sits on club fender.*)
STELLA. I couldn't. I came—oh—it was a sudden impulse. I'm still impulsive, you know.
DR. KIRBY. We thought you'd forgotten us.
STELLA. I've never forgotten you for a single moment. How could I? But I've been out of England for years—touring, working hard. My plans always seemed so confused. It was difficult to write.
DR. KIRBY. Yes, I can understand that, though in a quiet corner like this, we're apt to forget what the hustling and bustling world—*your* world—is like.
(STELLA *sits on pouf. He takes her hand for a moment.*)
You know, Stella, I've been thinking a lot just lately—— (*His voice trails away.*)
STELLA (*after a pause*). Yes, Father?
DR. KIRBY. Something happened that made me start thinking. You might call it taking stock. Thinking about life—my life—your life. You know, I've come to the conclusion that you were right, and your mother and I were wrong.
STELLA (*hastily, painfully*). No, no—— (*She rises and crosses to above table.*)

ACT I.] EDEN END. 25

Dr. Kirby. That's all right. (*Rising and following her, taking her by the shoulders.*) It's all old history now. We can talk frankly and freely now. And you're a grown-up woman, not a bit of a girl. (*He puts his cheek against hers.*) You were right to do what you did. (*Moving away* R.) I'm not saying that you didn't cause any pain——

Stella. I did, I know.

Dr. Kirby. But that wasn't your fault. That's life. Life can't move on without inflicting pain. We can't come into this world without somebody being hurt. As well I know. I shall be lucky if I don't see a bit more of it late to-night. (*He moves towards fire.*) The great cosmic processes have a habit of reaching a climax round here just when I've got comfortably off to sleep. (*He takes a further turn towards fire.*)

Stella. Poor Dad. Who is it this time?

Dr. Kirby. A Mrs. Sugden. I think she's since your time. Well, I think I've done my duty by her and her like in this neighbourhood for nearly forty years.

Stella. I know you have. And I'm sure they still worship you.

Dr. Kirby. Not they. I only wish they'd pay a bit more attention and then pay a f w more bills. But I'm not complaining. I've had a good life here. Your mother and I were happy. We'd all the friends we wanted. This has been a real home. Even to you, it was once.

Stella (*softly*). Do you think I could forget it?

Dr. Kirby. And then, besides my work and my family, I'd my little hobbies—my birds. (*With sudden animation.*) And by the way, don't let anybody tell you that you can't see a needle-tailed swift in this country, because I saw one myself, only this last summer. A needle-tailed swift. No mistake about it.

Stella (*going to* L. *of him affectionately, laughing and patting his shoulder*). Oh—Dad I won't let anybody tell me. I'll put them in their place at once.

Dr. Kirby. That's right. There's as much clap-trap talked about birds now as there is about anything else. Why, only the other day——

Stella (*laughing*). But, Dad, you can't go on about birds now. You were just going to tell me something important, something serious. (*She sits on left arm of chair, above fire.*)

Dr. Kirby (*between club fender and chair above fire, with a twinkle*). Well, this is important.

Stella. Yes, and I'd love to hear it, but that will do any time. Perhaps this other thing won't.

Dr. Kirby (*seriously*). That's true. This is something I wouldn't say to the younger children. What I was going to say was this. Looking back on my life, it's been a reasonably good one——

Stella. And you wouldn't change it.

Dr. Kirby. That's where you're wrong. I would.
Stella (*surprised*). Dad!
Dr. Kirby. There was a time when I had to make a choice.
Stella. Between this—and another kind of life?
Dr. Kirby. Yes. I wasn't always a plodding old G.P., you know, years behind the times.
(*He sits in chair above fire. She puts a hand on his shoulder.*)
Once, I was thought to be a very clever young man. I had a brilliant career as a student. Then I had to make a choice, between settling down here, quietly and comfortably, or taking a risk in London. I might have failed there. On the other hand, I might have been successful. Men who walked the hospitals when I did, men who hadn't the reputation I had, have been very successful. Some of them—I could give you their names—have been knighted, and so forth, are now rich and famous.
Stella. Pooh!—what's that!
Dr. Kirby. Mere vulgar rewards, if you like.
Stella. In Harley Street you'd never have seen a bird—except a dirty London sparrow.
Dr. Kirby. I'm not envying them, Stella. Nevertheless, they've had brilliant careers, done original work, met all the great personalities of their time, missed none of the prizes of life.
Stella. How do you know? They've missed the larks on Eden Moor.
Dr. Kirby. The larks and the moors are there if they want them, and they've probably more leisure now to enjoy such things than I have. And in addition, they've had all the rest. They've lived as I haven't lived, and as you—I'm glad to say—*are* living. You were right, Stella, to cut and run when you did. And now, looking back when it's all nearly ended——
Stella (*sharply*). Don't talk like that, Father. You're not old yet.
Dr. Kirby (*firmly*). I say, looking back when it's all nearly ended, I wish now that I'd had the same sort of courage.
Stella. It's not courage.
Dr. Kirby. I won't envy my—er—distinguished colleagues. (*He pats her hand.*) But I can envy you, my dear. And I do. You made a bolt for the main road. You're doing what you always wanted to do, and you've made a success of it, gone all over the world, been applauded and admired everywhere, given pleasure to thousands and thousands —
Stella (*jumping up in distress and crossing to above table*). Oh— Dad—please, please stop.
Dr. Kirby (*astonished*). What's the matter? I never knew actresses suffered from such modesty.
Stella (*trying to take hold of herself*). It isn't that.
Dr. Kirby. What is it, then?

ACT I.]   EDEN END.   27

STELLA. Oh—I don't know. Perhaps it's hearing *you* say these things.

DR. KIRBY. Don't try to be kind to me. It's the truth, and you know it.

STELLA (*bursting out*). It's—— (*Checks herself.*) Well, I suppose it's embarrassing. (*She crosses to fire.*)

DR. KIRBY. I can talk to you properly. I see you now as a grown-up person.

(STELLA *sits on chair below fire, picking up book, which is on chair, and putting it on floor beside it.*)

STELLA (*with irony*). Thank you, Dad.

DR. KIRBY. Ah well—it's not easy for a parent. I suppose I ought to see Lilian and Wilfred as grown-up people now, too, but I can't. Not only because they're younger than you, but because there hasn't been the same break. I ought to be frank with them, but it's difficult.

STELLA (*gravely*). You can be frank with me, then?

DR. KIRBY. Yes. I find it quite easy.

STELLA (*after an effort*). Then—then why did you talk about "looking back when it's all nearly ended"? You're not really old, you know.

DR. KIRBY. I'm not young.

STELLA (*relieved*). Oh—is that all?

DR. KIRBY. No, I'm afraid it isn't. There's something I can tell you that I can't tell the other two. You can stand it. They can't. You're older. You have your profession. You're enjoying life. You've really done with us. So you can stand it.

(STELLA *laughs bitterly.*)

What does that mean?

STELLA. Nothing. Go on. I can stand it. (*Suddenly alert, alarmed, she rises and goes over to him, kneeling beside him on his* R.) Dad—does this mean that there's something wrong with you—that you're ill?

DR. KIRBY. Take it easy, Stella. I'm afraid it does. (*Smiling.*) One advantage of being in my profession is that you get to know what's happening inside you. I've got a bad heart. I had a very nasty bout of influenza a few years ago, and I did a very silly thing, the sort of thing I've warned hundreds of people against doing. I got up and started work again far too early. So I landed myself with a bad heart.

STELLA. But—what's wrong with it?

DR. KIRBY (*easily*). A lot of things. It's worse than my old bike. But you might describe the trouble—shortly—as a valvular lesion with inefficient compensation.

STELLA. But, Dad . . .

DR. KIRBY. Oh—I do what I can about it, of course. I don't

work as hard as I used to do, though it's not easy to rest here. And I give myself digitalis—and other things. I get along—but——

STELLA. It's serious—then?

DR. KIRBY (*smiling*). No joke at all. In fact—I'm very glad you've come to see us now.

STELLA (*very distressed*). Dad!

DR. KIRBY. Easy, Stella. It seems a shabby trick landing you with this the minute you arrive, but I think you might have noticed something. And I'm telling you quite frankly so that you won't discuss it with Lilian and Wilfred. It's our little secret. Not much of one—but there you are.

STELLA (*rising*). I shan't say anything. (*She crosses to table and sits on upstage edge of it, fiddling with cards.*)

DR. KIRBY. That's right. They haven't settled down to their lives yet as you have to yours. In fact, I'm sometimes a bit worried about Lilian. I'm not grumbling about myself. I've had a good run. (*He rises and goes to fire.*) I'd like to live long enough to see this country settling down a bit better.

STELLA. Oh—bother the country, I don't care about that. It's you.

DR. KIRBY. Yes, but this has been a very unsettling, worrying year so far. Two big strikes. Ulster arming for rebellion. Young women being forcibly fed in gaol. This health insurance business. Everybody rushing about at thirty and forty miles an hour, up in the air as well as on the roads. Not much sunset calm about things. But in a year or two we may have settled down again. I like to think so.

STELLA (*in low voice*). I hope so—for your sake.

DR. KIRBY (*briskly*). Ah well—that's enough about me. Dismal stuff. (*Going towards her a little.*) I've got to hear about all your triumphs. Been all over the place, haven't you?

STELLA (*with forced animation*). Yes, all over. Like a crazy parcel.

DR. KIRBY. And enjoyed it, eh? Constant change, excitement, applause, eh? But don't let it spoil you.

STELLA (*with a little ironic smile*). I'll do my best, Dad. Unless I'm spoilt already.

DR. KIRBY. No sign of it. I was against you leaving home and going on the stage, but chiefly, I think, for your mother's sake. I believe it does girls good to go out into the world.

STELLA. Sometimes.

DR. KIRBY (*lowering voice*). I've never said anything to her—and of course I've been glad to have her here—but I've often thought that Lilian's been at home too long. She might have done a lot better for herself if she'd followed your example and found something she wanted to do away from home. Don't tell her that.

STELLA. I won't. But probably she stayed on simply because I went. For your sake.

Dr. Kirby (*heartily*). Oh no, I don't think so. I never asked her to stay. She likes being at home. A lot of girls do, of course. Quite natural. (*Looks at his watch.*) Must be nearly supper-time. Where's Lilian? (*He goes to door* c.—r. *of it.*)
Stella. I ought to be doing something.
Dr. Kirby. Nonsense. You're a guest. The work here's easy, and we've plenty to do it. Lilian and old Sarah—and a woman from the village comes in every day.

(Lilian *enters* c.)

Ah, Lilian, I was just wondering about supper. Stella must be hungry.
Lilian (l. *of him*). It'll be ready in about ten minutes.
Dr. Kirby. Good.

(*He goes out* c., *closing door behind him.*)

(Lilian *advances into the room.*)

Lilian (*going to window and drawing curtains*). Your room's ready now, if you want to go up. And Wilfred's taken your trunk upstairs. (*She turns up piano lamp.*)
Stella. Thanks, Lilian. I suppose I ought to go up. I'm probably filthy, but I've been too excited to care.
Lilian. You look all right.
Stella. We old travellers know all sorts of dodges. (*Stares at* Lilian.)
Lilian. What's the matter?
Stella. You know—you're different.
Lilian. Naturally. (*She crosses above* Stella *towards* r.) It's such a long time since you saw me last. (*She takes work basket from bookcase and puts it on pouf.*)
Stella (*going to her*). Are you happy?
Lilian (*rather impatiently*). I don't know. Isn't that—rather a silly question?
Stella. Is it?
Lilian. I think so. I mean, one isn't always asking oneself about happiness.
Stella. I am.
Lilian. Yes, you. You always were.
Stella. And whether you ask or not, after all, you always know whether you're happy or not.
Lilian (*rolling up darned socks*). Most of the time one isn't either happy or unhappy.
Stella. Like you—now?
Lilian. Like me—now.
Stella (*sitting* r. *of table*). But there's something about you I don't understand.
Lilian. Well, why bother?

STELLA (*taking her hands*). But, my dear, I want to bother. You talk as if we were strangers.

LILIAN. Aren't we ? (*She crosses to above table for socks.*) We haven't set eyes on one another for years.

STELLA. Yes, but I've been thinking about you all the time.

LILIAN. Even if you have, that's not enough. I'd only just left school when you went away. I'm quite different.

STELLA. I see that.

LILIAN. We'll get to know one another again—perhaps. But don't force it. (*She crosses above* STELLA *towards* R.)

(*As* LILIAN *passes,* STELLA *detains her momentarily with her left hand—which is un-gloved—*LILIAN *sees the mark where a wedding ring has been.*)

STELLA (*trying to smile*). And that's not meant for a snub, I hope ?

LILIAN (*gravely*). No. (*Crossing to pouf.*) Tell me something.

STELLA (*lightly*). Anything. (*She goes to her.*)

LILIAN (*in low voice*). You're married, aren't you ?

STELLA (*startled, but in low voice*). Yes. How did you know ?

LILIAN. I saw the mark of the ring.

(STELLA *stares at her left hand and rubs the ring finger.*)

STELLA (*troubled*). I'd probably have told you all—later. But please don't say anything—yet.

LILIAN. What happened ?

STELLA. I married three years ago—in Australia. He was an actor, in the same company. After the first year it didn't work—very well. We've separated now.

LILIAN. Where is he ?

STELLA. A week ago I couldn't have told you. We separated in America. But three days ago I called at my agent's in town—and I saw him there. We have the same agent. It was queer.

LILIAN. What's his name ?

STELLA. Charles Appleby. He's not famous or anything. Just a goodish actor. Very nice family. And he can be quite charming --at times. We were very happy together for a little while.

LILIAN. And now you're separated.

STELLA (*with a pitiful smile*). Yes. All bust up. (*She crosses to above table.*) Yes, I'm not really Stella Kirby any more, but Mrs. Charles Appleby, not living with her husband.

LILIAN. Is there going to be a divorce ?

STELLA. I don't know.

(*There is a ring heard off through door* C.)

It's all a muddle. (*Coming down* L. *to below table.*) Let's stop talking about it. And please, Lilian, don't say anything. We'll talk afterwards, if you like.

(*Voices are heard outside door up* C. STELLA *and* LILIAN *look towards it, the latter expectantly.* WILFRED *enters, followed by* GEOFFREY FARRANT *and* DR. KIRBY. FARRANT *is a fair brown-faced man in his late thirties, dressed in tweeds. There is still something of the regular officer in his appearance. He walks with a slight limp.* WILFRED *goes to piano,* FARRANT *to down* C. *and* DR. KIRBY *to chair below fire.*)

WILFRED. Stella, look who's here. Miss Kirby, this is Captain Farrant.

STELLA (*with animation*). Geoffrey! (*Holding out her hand.*)

(*They meet below and* R. *of table.*)

FARRANT. Stella! (*Shaking hands.*) This *is* a surprise. (*Turning, offhandedly.*) Hello, Lilian.

STELLA. You've hardly changed at all, Geoffrey. How have you managed it?

FARRANT (*pleased and shy*). Oh—I don't know—quiet life—plenty of exercise, riding—that sort of thing. (*Looking at her, smilingly.*) You've not changed much yourself, you know.

STELLA. Not much! I suppose that really means I'm looking a hag?

(LILIAN *goes to fire.*)

FARRANT. Of course it doesn't. Anything but—— Matter of fact, you're looking prettier than ever. Isn't she, Dr. Kirby?

STELLA. Well, it's terribly nice seeing you again, Geoffrey. And so soon, too. I'd hardly hoped for that. And still living at the old place, too.

FARRANT. Yes, still at the old place. It's mine now, you know.

STELLA (*sitting on chair* R. *of table—leaning over back of it*). Do you remember the birthday party you had, just after your leg got better, and we let that enormous pig loose from the farm?

FARRANT (*laughing*). Good Lord, yes. Do you remember that?

STELLA. Of course I do. I remember everything. And that time when old Birtley got so drunk when the beagles were meeting at your house?

WILFRED (*dropping down* L. *of table*). By Jove, I remember that.

FARRANT. I should think you do. So do I. Poor old Birtley. I say, Stella, we *have* got something to talk about. It's going to take us days——

LILIAN (*cutting in*). Supper will be ready in a few minutes. I'll ask Sarah to tell you. (*She moves to door up* C.)

DR. KIRBY. Why, where are *you* going, Lilian?

LILIAN (*shortly*). I'm going to bed. I don't want any supper. I've got a headache. Good night.

(*She goes out quickly up* C.)

FARRANT (*after a pause, moving up* C.). Oh, I say—poor old Lilian.

DR. KIRBY. Didn't know she wasn't feeling well.

WILFRED (*carelessly*). She'll be all right. Just one of her moods. She's very queer sometimes. Best to leave her alone.

FARRANT. Excitement, perhaps. Stella coming back, eh?

WILFRED. I say, Stella, did you see " Gipsy Love " at Daly's? I did. Been trying to play bits ever since. I've got the music of some of the new musical comedies. You're just the person I wanted. Come and play some of them.

STELLA. What, now?

WILFRED. Why not? Just a minute or two.

FARRANT. Go on, Stella. Fine to see you at the piano again.

STELLA (*laughing*). All right. (*She rises, goes over and sits at piano.*)

(WILFRED *goes below*, FARRANT *above piano.*)

WILFRED. Try this one. It's called " The Pink Lady."

(STELLA *begins playing with* WILFRED *standing by the piano and* FARRANT *looking on admiringly;* DR. KIRBY *is seated, beating time.* SARAH *opens door* C. *and stands in doorway, smiling.*)

SLOW CURTAIN.

ACT II

SCENE.—*Same as Act I.*

TIME.—*Afternoon four days later.*

WILFRED *is discovered. He is very uneasy. He approaches the telephone, hesitates, listens, then goes to door up* C., *looks to see if anybody is about, closes the door and comes back to telephone, looks up number in pocket-book, reaches out as if to take off the receiver and then hesitates again. Finally he comes away from it to below table, sits on table, and picks up a copy of "Punch" that is lying on the table. Then the telephone bell rings. He dashes off to the telephone, obviously in high hopes.*
There is the sound of wind, off.

WILFRED (*at telephone, eagerly*). Yes? Yes? Hello. Yes? (*Is obviously disappointed.*) Oh—Dr. Philips. No, Dad—Dr. Kirby —isn't back yet. Yes, I'll see him, I expect. . . . Yes, in a few minutes. . . . At your house—Monday afternoon, three o'clock. I'll tell him. Good-bye. (*He rings off and goes back and sits again on downstage edge of table, reading "Punch."*)

(*As he leaves the telephone,* SARAH *enters from* R.)

SARAH (*crossing above table to window*). It'll be teeming down afore so long.
WILFRED (*gloomily*). Well, let it.
SARAH. Did Miss Stella take her mackintosh?
WILFRED. I don't know. I expect so.
SARAH. She'll want it.
WILFRED. You ought to see it rain in Africa.
SARAH (*coming to* L. *of him*). Does it rain there an' all?
WILFRED. Of course it does.
SARAH. Well, I remember young Greenhead—the butcher's lad who went out to fight Kruger—telling me it never rained at all. All dry and dusty, he said it was. Never a drop o' water.
WILFRED. That's a different part of Africa. That's South Africa.
SARAH. Where are you then?
WILFRED. West Africa. Two thousand miles away. Quite different. Very hot and wet. Millions of blacks.
SARAH. Eh, fancy! And it only seems a week since you wor a little lad.

WILFRED. It's years since. And anyhow, what's that got to do with it, Sarah, you old chump?

SARAH. A lot more nor you think. (*She crosses below table to fire, to poke it.*) But then, lads has no sense. And they don't get owerloaded with it when they stop being lads. You can't stir up in the doctor's room for daft old birds' eggs.

WILFRED (*accusingly*). Sarah, you've broken some more.

SARAH (*turning to him, poker in hand*). Only two. You can't move for 'em, and if you so much as look at 'em, they break. (*She replaces poker.*)

WILFRED (*crossing to* L. *of her*). You've gone and broken the only two specimens of the egg of the Great Spotted Gofoozle we have in the country.

SARAH. How do you know? You didn't see 'em.

WILFRED. I shall tell him.

SARAH. Master Wilfred, if you do that——

(*They both smile.*)

But you wouldn't, would you? You see, if you say nowt, he never misses 'em, for he's more eggs nor he knows what to do with. So long as he thinks they're all there, he's contented.

(*The wind dies away.*)

WILFRED (*going above her to fire*). You're a wicked old woman.

SARAH. If you start telling on me, I'll tell on you.

WILFRED. Blackmail, that is. Besides, you've nothing to tell.

SARAH. What about them three cigars I saw you take?

WILFRED (*laughs*). Three cigars? Why, that's ages ago. At least seven years. Dad wouldn't care now. (*Listens.*) I think he's here, isn't he?

SARAH. Yes. I heard him. (*Going to door up* C.) Nobody can say I'm hard o' hearing. I can still hear a lot better nor some of you. I'll ask him if he wants owt.

(*She goes out* C.)

(WILFRED *sits* R. *of table and settles down with "Punch."*)

(DR. KIRBY *comes in* C. *wearing an overcoat.*)

DR. KIRBY (*coming down to above table*). Hello, Wilfred, any messages for me? (*He puts his hat on table and starts opening two letters.*)

WILFRED. Yes. Dr. Philips of Martinbro just rang up to say that there'd be a meeting at his house next Monday afternoon at three.

DR. KIRBY. Next Monday at three? Well, I've no doubt some of us will be there, if our patients will let us.

WILFRED. What's it about? Health Insurance?

DR. KIRBY. Yes. Where are the girls this afternoon?

WILFRED. Geoffrey Farrant called for Stella, and they've gone out for a walk. And Lilian went out somewhere, I don't know where, about quarter of an hour ago. And I'm here, looking at " Punch."

DR. KIRBY (*crossing to fire and sitting on club fender*). So I see. Good number?

WILFRED. Not so far. I don't see the point of some of these jokes. (*Turning pages.*) This, for instance. (*Reads.*) Candid Friend (to M.F.H.) : " I don't think much of your cubhunters, Jack." M.F.H. : " They're very useful horses ; you see, we can either ride 'em or eat 'em." What's the point of that?

DR. KIRBY. No idea. I'll have to look at the drawing.

(WILFRED *rises and crosses to his father to show him.* DR. KIRBY *gives an expression of not seeing it.* WILFRED *returns to* R. *of table.*)

WILFRED (*turning pages*). And here's another. Officer (visiting outpost) : " If you saw one of the enemy, what would you do ? " Sentry : " I calls 'im to 'alt." Officer : " Suppose he won't halt ? " Sentry (with relish) : " I takes and 'unts 'im wiv me bayonnit." I don't think that's very funny. (*He sits* R. *of table.*)

DR. KIRBY. It wouldn't be very funny for the enemy. I saw some photographs of bayonet wounds once.

WILFRED. My hat, no. I shouldn't like anybody after me with a bayonet.

DR. KIRBY (*picking up* " *Yorkshire Post* " *from downstage end of club fender*). Well, I shouldn't worry. It isn't very likely that anybody will be. The world's got a lot more sense than it's given credit for in the newspapers. And it's got science now to help it.

WILFRED. Dad.

DR. KIRBY. Yes.

WILFRED. Are you sorry I didn't go in for something scientific? That I'm not a doctor, for instance?

DR. KIRBY. Not if you're happy as you are.

WILFRED. Well, I don't know that I'm *happy*.

DR. KIRBY (*hastily*). I didn't mean that. Silly word. Reasonably contented, let us say.

WILFRED. Well, it's not bad, you know.

DR. KIRBY. After all, you're seeing the world. More than I've ever done.

WILFRED (*hesitantly*). Yes. Only I don't seem to belong anywhere. I don't seem to belong to this place any more, and yet I can't really fit in with West Africa—nobody could.

DR. KIRBY. Well, that shouldn't bother you at your age. And after all, you've plenty of time. Years and years and years.

WILFRED (*hopefully*). Yes, that's true. Do you often wonder what you'll be like in ten years' time?

DR. KIRBY (*dryly*). Not often, no.

WILFRED. No, of course, naturally you wouldn't.
DR. KIRBY (*grimly amused*). Oh? Why?
WILFRED. Well, being older—you're completely settled, aren't you? You've always been here and——
DR. KIRBY. And I always will be, eh? You talk as if I wasn't so much perishable human stuff, just like yourself, but the Cow Rock up there on Eden moorside. (*He rises.*) I suppose that's how I seem. I was here, all complete, when you arrived, and I'll simply go on and on. That's the result of being a parent. You're an institution, not a human being. (*He drops paper on chair below fire.*)
WILFRED. I wouldn't mind if I was a bit more of an institution, Dad. Everything seems to slide away from me all the time. And I never seem to be in the right place.
DR. KIRBY (*briskly*). Partly liver, and partly boredom.

(*A bell rings off.*)

You ought to be having a sharp walk now. (*He crosses to above table, patting* WILFRED'S *shoulder as he passes: then he picks up his hat.*) By the way, now that Stella's here—and looks like stopping a few weeks—I think we might entertain a bit more, don't you?
WILFRED. Good idea. If you can find anybody worth entertaining.
DR. KIRBY. Shouldn't be impossible. Just think of some people —young people, the sort Stella would like—we could have.

(SARAH *appears at door up* C. *and comes to* R. *of* DR. KIRBY.)

What is it, Sarah? Do you want me?
SARAH (*handing him note*). That little lad o' Mrs. Hepple's brought it.
DR. KIRBY (*glancing at it*). All right. I'll call. Back in about an hour or so, Wilfred, if anybody wants me.

(*He goes out* C.)

(SARAH *stands aside to let him pass and shuts door.* WILFRED *has put his feet up on table:* SARAH *comes to above table and lifts them off.*)

SARAH (*after waiting a moment*). Now I'll tell you what it is——
WILFRED (*still reading "Punch"*). Oh shut up, Sarah. I want to read.
SARAH (*offended*). That's a nice way to talk, isn't it?
WILFRED. No. But I want to be quiet.
SARAH (*moving slowly above him to* C. *on her way to door* R.). I've seen the time when you'd have got a good slap from me for answering back like that. But now you're a big lad and I'm an old woman. Yes, and I know what you're telling yourself—a silly old woman. (*Getting nearer to door* R.) Well, old I may be, but I'm not so silly as some folk think——

WILFRED (*deliberately*). I want to read. (*He puts his feet up again.*)

SARAH (*a parting shot*). And a lot o' good it'll do you.

(*She goes out* R., *closing door behind her.*)

(WILFRED *looks up, looking at both doors, then gets up. He is rather indecisive. He moves over to the telephone, then stretches out a hand for the instrument, hesitates, rings it and listens.*)

(SARAH *opens the door* R.)

(*At door, with malicious triumph.*) I thought you wanted to read.

WILFRED (*slamming down receiver, startled and angry, shouting*). What's it got to do with you what I want to do?

SARAH (*going to fire*). That's not reading, playing about with that thing.

WILFRED (*not so loud*). That's my business.

SARAH. You've been wanting to get at it on the quiet, half the day. I've seen you. And not for the first time neither. And if you'd any sense you'd let it alone.

WILFRED. You don't know what you're talking about.

SARAH. Oh yes—I do. It may be all right for the doctor—folk being poorly and in a hurry—but no good'll come to you, talking down that thing. (*Getting to* R. *of him.*) If it's worth saying, it's worth saying properly, instead o' gabbling into a daft machine. And if you thought anything o' the lass——

WILFRED (*sulkily*). How do you know it is a lass—as you call it?

SARAH. You wouldn't be making such a palaver if it worn't a lass.

(WILFRED *goes to window.*)

And she can't be up to so much when you've got to keep so quiet about her. Leave her alone, I say, and that telly-machine with her.

(*There is a noise of front door closing.*)

WILFRED. Oh—rats! And there's somebody coming now. You *are* a nuisance, Sarah.

SARAH. It'll be Miss Lilian.

(SARAH *goes to fire and pokes it.* WILFRED *goes to above and* L. *of table. The door* C. *is opened by* CHARLES APPLEBY, *who comes in, quite at ease.* SARAH *turns from fire to look at him. He is a man about forty, probably wearing rather loud Harris tweeds, very much the actor in the country. At this moment he is also wearing a very large ulster, which is spotted with rain. There are signs that he drinks too much. The evidence of breeding and charm is still there, but it is doubtful how much longer it will be there. He pauses at door, comes to* C. *and smiles at both. He flicks rain off the lapels of his coat.*)

CHARLES (*smiling*). Beginning to rain. What a lot of rain we've had this autumn, haven't we ?
WILFRED (*gaping at him*). Yes.
SARAH. Have you come to see Dr. Kirby ?
CHARLES (*enjoying himself*). Not particularly. (*To* WILFRED.) Now I'm not quite sure about you. But (*to* SARAH) I know who you are. You're Sarah.
SARAH. Well, what if I am ?
CHARLES. Recognized you at once, you see. Heard a lot about you.
SARAH. Well, I've never set eyes on you before, young man.
CHARLES (*to* WILFRED). Not quite sure about you. Can't place you. But perhaps you're not one of the family here.
WILFRED. Yes I am. I'm Wilfred Kirby.
CHARLES (*smiling*). Of course. Well, I'm one of the family, too.
SARAH. That you're not.
CHARLES. Sorry, but I am. I'm Charlie Appleby.

(*A look between* SARAH *and* WILFRED.)

SARAH. We're no wiser now.
CHARLES. This won't do. (*Turns and opens door up* C., *calling*.) I say—er, Lilian—Lilian—you'd better come and introduce me.

(*Another look between* SARAH *and* WILFRED.)

They don't know anything about me in here. We're all very embarrassed.
WILFRED. I say, is this a joke ?
CHARLES (*coming in from door and standing* R. *of it*). Not much of one, old boy. (*Turning*.) Here's Lilian.

(*Enter* LILIAN *by door* C., *and stands* L. *of it*.)

LILIAN. Wilfred, this is Mr.——
CHARLES. Whoa, stop ! Not Mr.—just Appleby, Charlie Appleby —Charlie.
LILIAN (*rather grimly*). He's our brother-in-law. Stella's husband.
SARAH (*moving forward a step or two*). Never !
CHARLES. Sorry. Know how you feel, Sarah.
WILFRED. But look here—when—when did this happen ?
CHARLES. Three years ago. In Australia. Let's complete the ceremony of introduction, shall we ? (*Holds out a hand and crosses to* WILFRED *to shake hands—below* LILIAN.) How do you do ?
WILFRED (*laughing nervously and shaking hands*). How do you do ?
CHARLES (*then crossing to* L. *of* SARAH *and holding out a hand*). Sarah.
SARAH (*moving forward uncertainly*). And you really are Miss Stella's husband ?

ACT II.] EDEN END. 39

CHARLES (*stooping down to her*). Mrs. Stella's husband. Yes.
SARAH (*bewildered and suspicious*). But she's never said a single word to me about it, not a single word. I can't understand it.
LILIAN (*rather sharply*). Just a minute, Sarah. I want you to help me.

(*She moves to door* C. *and goes off.* SARAH *follows slowly, going below* CHARLES *to door* C., *with a puzzled and suspicious look at him. She gives him a final look, before closing door. The latter notices it.*)

CHARLES. The poor old girl is convinced I'm an impostor. And I must say I never felt so much like one before.
WILFRED. But, you see, we didn't know anything about it.
CHARLES (*dryly*). No, I've gathered that.
WILFRED. She's been home four days, and never said a word.

(*Pause.* CHARLES *throws his hat on chair below fire.*)

CHARLES. Didn't know how to break the news, I expect. Difficult, sometimes. I'm not a good newsbreaker myself.

(*Another pause.*)

WILFRED (*going to* L. *of table*). Are you on the stage, too?
CHARLES (*throwing gloves on chair below fire*). Such is fame. Am I on the stage?
WILFRED. I'm sorry—but——
CHARLES. Don't apologize. I expect you lead a quiet life. It looks a quiet life, from the little I've seen of it.
WILFRED. Oh—I'm only home on leave. From Africa.
CHARLES. Soldier?
WILFRED. No, I'm with the British West African Trading Company.
CHARLES. This family gets about a bit, doesn't it? And why I'm still wearing this damned thing, I don't know.

(CHARLES *gets to* C., *back to audience, and begins taking off his ulster.* WILFRED *comes to below table to* L. *of him, to help him. He puts the coat on piano-stool.* CHARLES *turns and reveals his watch-chain and crosses round below table, up* L. *of it to* L. *of* WILFRED, *who is above table.*)

I've been on the stage twenty years. Ran away from Oxford to go on the stage. Been all over, played nearly everything. Juvenile leads. Character parts now. Soon I'll be doing the heavies. What a life!
WILFRED. Don't you like it?
CHARLES. Never been able to decide. Do you like Africa?
WILFRED. I'm not sure.

(CHARLES *digs him in the ribs and goes to window. They both laugh.*)

I say, are you staying here?
CHARLES. Looks like it, doesn't it?

WILFRED. I hope you are.

CHARLES. Why?

WILFRED. Well, we might go round a bit. Unless you want to be with Stella all the time.

CHARLES (*dryly*). No, I don't think I shall want to be with Stella all the time, old boy. Certainly let's go round a bit. I can't imagine where we'll go (*turning to window*), but no doubt you know where the lads of the village—the ber-hoys, the ker-nuts—disport themselves. (*Going up to* L. *of* WILFRED, *above table.*) I don't suppose you come all the way from West Africa simply to watch the rain dripping off the old stone walls—do you?

WILFRED. Rather not.

CHARLES (*sitting on upstage edge of table, back to audience.*) You must take me round, you must show me the sights, and we'll see if we can't have some fun. I've never been to a place yet—and I've been to some dam' rum places—where one couldn't have some fun if one tried.

WILFRED. I'll do my best for you.

CHARLES (*yawning*). Matter of fact, you're a find. I'd forgotten about you. I saw myself simply having some grim chats about appendicitis in the surgery with your governor. What's he like by the way?

WILFRED. Oh—Dad's all right.

CHARLES. To tell you the truth, I wasn't looking forward to meeting him. After all, it's a bit thick suddenly having a son-in-law thrust on you. Actor, too. Greasy hair, dirty collar. No money. Probably a bad lot.

WILFRED (*enthusiastically*). I think it's going to be fun, having you here.

CHARLES. Thank God somebody thinks so. But I'm not in good form at the moment. Feel half dead. Got up too early to catch that train. And what a train!

(LILIAN *enters by door up* C.)

I'm just saying I feel half dead after that train.

LILIAN (*going to bookcase, below fire, in search of a book*). I hope you don't mind a camp bed.

CHARLES (*rising*). Not at all, so long as it isn't the kind that tries to fold itself up again in the middle of the night.

WILFRED. No, it's all right. But, look here, you can have my bed and I'll have the camp bed.

LILIAN. Well, you can settle it between you, because I've put him in your room, Wilfred.

WILFRED. Good. (*Hesitates, then goes down to* L. *of* LILIAN). Though—I say—oughtn't he to be—you know?

LILIAN (*crossing below* WILFRED *up to door* C. *with* CHARLES's *gloves and hat, which she gives him, briskly*). That's all right. I'm running this house.

CHARLES (*picking up coat from piano-stool and taking hat and gloves from* LILIAN). Running it very well, too, I should think. I'd like to turn in for an hour if nobody's any objection.

LILIAN. No, I expect you're tired. Are you hungry?

CHARLES. No, thanks. I'm not hungry. But I'm devilish thirsty. Could I have a drink?

LILIAN. Would you like some tea?

CHARLES (*with mock gravity*). Sorry, but it doesn't agree with me. If there's such a thing as a whisky and soda going——

WILFRED. There's some in the dining-room.

LILIAN (*moving to door* C.). Come along. And I'll show you where your room is. Then I must go out again.

(*She goes out by door* C.)

CHARLES (*following her, putting his hat on his head*). I'll take my drink up to my room and not be in anybody's way.

(CHARLES *goes through door* C. *and off* R.)

(WILFRED *follows them. The room is darker now. The rain and wind can be heard. After a moment* WILFRED *returns, putting on a mackintosh and a cap. He closes the door after him, carefully, then goes to the telephone nervously. He takes off the receiver and rings. He is very nervous, and catches his breath as he talks.*)

WILFRED (*at telephone*). Hello . . . I want Denly two-six. . . . Hello, is that Denly two-six? Is that the "White Hart"? . . . Could I speak to Miss Alice Murgatroyd, please? . . . Oh, but you could get her, couldn't you? . . . It's—er—a friend. . . . Yes, it's important. . . . Oh, thanks very much. . . . Oh (*gasps*), is that you, Alice? It's Wilfred . . . (*Louder.*) Wilfred you know—Wilfred Kirby . . . (*Disappointed.*) Didn't you recognize my voice? . . . Oh, I see. . . . Do you remember the other night? Listen, can I see you to-day? . . . Oh no, it isn't the same thing at all seeing you in the bar. . . . But I must see you alone . . . please, Alice. . . . Oh . . . (*Disappointed.*) But listen, if you don't go on duty until seven, I could see you before then. I'd come over at once. . But you can't have so much to do. (*Joyfully.*) Oh, good. I'll come over at once on my bike. . . .

(*The wind can be heard very loud now.*)

(*Desperately again.*) No, honestly, it isn't raining (*looking through window*) much. It's nothing. Really. And it'll probably be all over by the time I get there. . . . All right. At the bridge, eh? Oh, but you must be there. . . . Hello, hello.

(*He puts down the receiver, rings off and puts trouser-clips on, placing his foot on arm of chair above fire to do this. He then goes up to door* C., *but hears voices; so after one glance in that direction he hurries out through door* R. *The room now is almost dark.*)

(*The door up* c. *opens and* STELLA *and* FARRANT *come in, both wearing wet overcoats or mackintoshes.* STELLA *goes to* R. *of table,* FARRANT *comes to* R. *of her.*)

STELLA. Nobody in, thank goodness. We can still go on talking. Will you light the lamp?

FARRANT. Yes. And it won't be the first time I've done it here, either. (*He strikes a match and lights the standard lamp.*) Aren't you awfully wet?

STELLA. Wettish. (*Takes off her coat.*) I think we'd better put our coats in the nursery to dry. Give me yours.

(*The sound of rain gradually dies away.*)

FARRANT (*taking off his*). No, I'll take them both in. Give me yours.

(*The wind increases for a moment.*)

(FARRANT *takes the coats into room* R. STELLA *draws the curtains across the window, goes to fire and warms her feet. She is dressed now in country clothes, different from those in Act I. Then she hums a tune. She is obviously happy.*)

(*Returning and going to fire—below her.*) Nice in here after the rain outside. Looks—cosy.

STELLA (*laughs*). That's very elderly of you, Geoffrey.

FARRANT. I don't see that. Always like to be cosy after I've been out. Did when I was a boy. This is when a pipe tastes its best, indoors after the wind and the rain. (*Holds up his pipe.*) Do you mind?

STELLA. I've told you before. I adore your pipe. I think I'll smoke, too. Have you a cigarette for me, please?

FARRANT. Yes, of course.

(*He holds out a case. She takes one.*)

STELLA (*holding up the cigarette, smiling*). Do you mind?

FARRANT. I admit I *have* objected to women smoking, in my time. But I don't mind when you do it.

STELLA. You mean, it doesn't matter if a tough old hag like me takes to such bad habits?

FARRANT. Don't talk such rot, Stella. You're prettier than ever. And there never was anybody less *tough*—as you call it.

STELLA. You're becoming suspiciously neat at this sort of thing, Geoffrey, much better than you used to be. You've had lots of practice while I've been away.

(*He lights her cigarette, and then lights his pipe.* STELLA *sits above fire. The wind is noticeable.*)

Well, the walk didn't last long, and there was too much rain—but I loved it.

FARRANT. That's good.

STELLA. The rain suits this country here.

FARRANT. Good thing it does. We get plenty of it.

STELLA (*dreamily*). I wonder if you can understand what it means to come back after being so long away.

FARRANT. Of course I can. (*Sitting below fire.*) I was away over two years during the Boer War. Don't forget that.

STELLA. No, I'm not. But I've been away much longer than that. It seems centuries. Dirty provincial towns. Dozens of 'em. Stuffy little dressing-rooms. Stage doors down back streets.

FARRANT. Sounds beastly. Marvel to me how you stuck it.

STELLA. Then London. The real London. Cheap digs in Victoria and Paddington. Meals in teashops. Fog for days and days. No space, no fresh air.

FARRANT. But it was better when you went away touring?

STELLA. Yes, we saw a lot. Some of the places were lovely. And some—weren't. But, my dear, there was nothing like this anywhere.

FARRANT. There isn't, you know, if it's your own country.

STELLA (*ecstatically*). The grey stone walls climbing up the moors, Geoffrey. The little streams dashing down. The ling and the bracken. The green, green fields. The huge dark brooding hills. That heathery, salty, fresh smell. Oh—lovely, lovely. I feel like someone who's just been let out of prison. I'm alive again. You don't read poetry, do you, Geoffrey?

(*The wind effect fades away.*)

FARRANT (*apologetically*). Not much. Kipling, y'know. But can't get on with most of the others.

STELLA. Well, there are two lines of Wordsworth's that give me this country as nothing else does. I've repeated them over and over again—and they've always brought me back home here.

FARRANT. Good for them! What are they?

STELLA. They're at the very end of some ridiculous poem about a young shepherd coming into an estate. I remember the two lines that come before, so I'll put them in too. (*Quoting, giving the last two lines with deep feeling.*)

> "Love had he found in huts where poor men lie;
> His daily teachers had been woods and rills;
> The silence that is in the starry sky,
> The sleep that is among the lonely hills."

FARRANT (*sitting forward*). Say the last bit again.

STELLA. "The silence that is in the starry sky,
The sleep that is among the lonely hills."

FARRANT (*thoughtfully*). I get what he's driving at there, y'know. That's Wordsworth, is it? I must tackle him again.

(STELLA *laughs.*)

What's the joke?

STELLA. I suddenly saw you—in that den of yours at the Manor —tackling Wordsworth.
FARRANT (*after short laugh*). You can understand why I stay on at the old place—— (*He rises and relights pipe with a spill.*)
STELLA. Heavens, yes.
FARRANT. There isn't really a lot to do, looking after the estate, and sometimes I've told myself I'm a slacker, just hanging on there, doing a bit of hunting and shooting. I'd have been glad to have stayed in the army, of course, but my leg made that impossible. And, somehow, I've never been attracted to anything else. Probably because I don't want to leave the old place.
STELLA. You must never leave it.

(FARRANT *sits again.*)

You know, these last few days, I've been thinking again of my childhood. Things—oh, dozens of things—I'd forgotten have suddenly come back.
FARRANT. Do you like that?
STELLA. Yes. Even though some of the things are unhappy things.
FARRANT. I hope I wasn't one of 'em.
STELLA. No, you come in afterwards, Geoffrey. When I was growing up—or when I thought I was growing up. When I was (*in absurd tone*) a girl.
FARRANT. You're still a girl.
STELLA. My dear man, don't be ridiculous. I'm a woman. Very soon—horrors—I shall be an *old girl.*
FARRANT. That puts me well into the decayed class, then, for I'm older than you.
STELLA. It's different for a man. You're merely coming within sight of maturity.
FARRANT. I hope I'm maturing well.
STELLA. You're maturing beautifully, Geoffrey.
FARRANT. Nevertheless, you've changed, and I haven't.
STELLA. How have I changed? (*Hastily.*) If it's something unpleasant, don't tell me. I won't have to-day spoilt.
FARRANT. It isn't unpleasant.
STELLA. Go on, then, and tell me all about it.
FARRANT. When I've thought about you——
STELLA. Oh, have you thought about me?
FARRANT (*gravely*). I've thought about you a lot. Wondered where you were, what you were doing, and so on, and I've always thought that after being on the stage you'd be much harder. Harder, that is, than you used to be.
STELLA. And I was hard enough to you, wasn't I? Poor Geoffrey. I was a nasty, cocky, little beast.
FARRANT. No, you weren't. But you led me an awful dance sometimes, didn't you?
STELLA. I did. And now I apologize for it. Never mind,

Geoffrey. I treated ydu very badly, and you've been well revenged since.

FARRANT. Oh? How? Who by?

STELLA. Don't look so alarmed. I mean by—well—life. I thought I knew everything then. I knew nothing, and when that fact was forced upon me, it hurt. But go on. You thought I'd be harder still.

FARRANT. Yes. And you're not. You're—you know I'm no good at this sort of thing.

STELLA (*gently*). You're much better than you think you are. Besides, I've had the misfortune to meet a lot of men who prided themselves on being good at this sort of thing.

FARRANT. All blighters, I'll bet.

STELLA. Yes, Geoffrey. Mostly blighters.

FARRANT. What I meant to say was, that you're still yourself—Stella—but you're nicer, kinder—dash it, I'll say it—gentler than you used to be. At least to me you are.

STELLA. I'm glad you think so. I should like to be. I've learnt a good deal these last eight years. I've often thought how badly I treated you in the old days here. And I've been ashamed. Sometimes, just lately, I've been tempted to write and tell you so. But I didn't know what had happened to you. You might easily have forgotten all about me.

FARRANT (*in a low voice*). I've tried hard enough.

STELLA. I can understand that.

FARRANT. I wanted to get on with my own life. You'd got on with yours. That's reasonable, isn't it?

STELLA. Yes. And I should think that's what was the matter with it. Too reasonable.

FARRANT. Yes, too reasonable. I knew that the moment I came in here, the other night, and saw you again. I hadn't been doing badly the last year or two.

STELLA. At forgetting me?

FARRANT. Yes. I'd even been able to come here a good deal —sometimes to see your father, and Wilfred when he was on leave, but chiefly to see Lilian. I've seen a lot of her, you know.

STELLA. Yes, I gathered that.

FARRANT (*rising*). Lilian's a fine girl, you know. (*He knocks out his pipe on grate.*)

STELLA. I'm sure she is. That sounds absurd, doesn't it, when I'm her sister. But the fact is, I don't know her very well now. She's grown-up, and she's changed in the process, I suppose. But I'm sure there's something very strong and fine about her. She always had more courage and strength and honesty than I had.

(*As he is about to protest.*)

No, I mean that. (*She rises.*) Do you think I don't know myself now? I'm changeable, I'm weak, and I'm a coward. (*She throws her cigarette away into fire.*)

FARRANT. You're not.

STELLA. You don't know, my dear. I'm being weak and cowardly at this very moment.

FARRANT. I don't believe you.

STELLA (*almost in tears, but smiling*). I don't want you to believe me. (*Smiling at him.*) Dear Geoffrey.

(*She puts her hand out to him. He takes it.*)

FARRANT. You may be changeable. I don't know. But I know this. I'm not changeable. I loved you years ago. I love you now, just the same. I see why nobody's ever meant anything all this time. It's because of you. There's only you. I love you, Stella.

(*He looks down at her. She raises her face to him and he kisses her. Then she rests her head against his sleeve, closing her eyes. Nothing is said.*)

I may not be able to read poetry, Stella, but I've imagined that— over and over again.

STELLA (*with a tiny smile*). I've thought of it too—sometimes.

FARRANT. By Jove, have you? If I'd known that I'd have come charging all over Australia and the United States looking for you. See what I've missed.

(*He threatens to kiss her again, but she holds up a hand and shakes her head.*)

No, probably you're right. Now we've got to talk.

STELLA (*sitting above fire*). Yes, but not the kind of talk you mean, Geoffrey. No plans, no arrangements, no time tables, no— " seeing how we stand." Nothing like that.

FARRANT (*bewildered*). Oh! (*He sits on club fender.*)

STELLA. Just idle, foolish talk that gets you nowhere, that means nothing and yet can mean everything. It doesn't matter now who we are or how we stand, or anything like that. Just think of the two of us here, in a cosy little room, lost in the moorland rain. We're lost too. There isn't anybody else. Just us. And time's stopped for us. (*Dreamily.*) It flies at a terrible speed really, Geoffrey.

FARRANT. Oh, I don't know. Things don't change much.

STELLA. They do. Even in ten years' time—in Nineteen Twenty-two——

FARRANT. We shall only be in our forties.

STELLA. I know. And yet everything may be different. You never know. We might look back at this year and see it—oh! a thousand years away. In another world, a lost world.

FARRANT. But somehow or other things don't change much here.

STELLA. Yes, they do. I haven't been away so long, yet it's all different really. Mother gone. Wilfred and Lilian grown-up—

ACT II.] EDEN END. 47

half strangers. Father much older—too old. I sound like Stevenson's Wanderer. Do you remember the verse I used to keep saying over and over again ? (*She repeats the verse beginning "Home was home then, my dear," very softly.*)

"Home was home then, my dear, full of kindly faces.
Home was home then, my dear, happy for the child.
Fire and the windows bright glittered on the moorland.
Song, tuneful song, built a palace in the wild."

(*Just before the end the door* C. *opens quietly and* CHARLES *stands there, looking like a man who has just had a nap.* FARRANT *stares at him in surprise. Then, with a gesture, he calls* STELLA'S *attention to him. When* STELLA *sees him she gives a sharp cry, rises, and stands with a hand pressed against her heart.* FARRANT *also rises.* CHARLES *comes to* L. *of* STELLA.)

CHARLES. Sorry if I startled you, Stella, but I didn't want to interrupt the performance.

STELLA (*with an enormous effort*). Charles ?

CHARLES (*cheerfully*). Didn't they tell you I was coming ? Too bad. Wanted to make a surprise of it, I suppose. Something to pass the long autumn evening.

STELLA. But how did you get here ?

CHARLES. Train, my dear. Train from town. Hours and hours and hours of it, and started about dawn. I'm feeling a bit muzzy too. (*Indicating* FARRANT, *who is standing rigid.*) I'm afraid we're embarrassing your friend—this gentleman. Hadn't you better introduce me ?

STELLA (*silent a moment, then making a big effort*). Geoffrey, this is Charles Appleby—my husband. Captain Farrant.

CHARLES. How d'you do ? An old friend of my wife's, I expect. Think I've heard her mention you. (*Looks shrewdly from one to the other.*) If you'll excuse me one minute, I'll go and get myself a drink. Always get thirsty on trains, most curious thing.

(*He goes out.*)

(FARRANT *stares at* STELLA.)

FARRANT. Is this true ?
STELLA. Yes.
FARRANT. But why didn't you tell me ?
STELLA (*with a miserable smile*). I told you I was weak and cowardly, didn't I ?
FARRANT (*contemptuously*). Yes, but I didn't know it was as bad as that.
STELLA. Please, Geoffrey, don't try to hurt me. I'm hurt enough as it is.
FARRANT. What about me ? I suppose you think I'm enjoying myself.

STELLA (*in tears*). Please, Geoffrey. It isn't as bad as it seems. We were married three years ago. We've been separated for nearly a year now. (*Crossing* L. *to above table.*) I don't know why he's here. I didn't ask him here.

FARRANT. I don't think I want to hear any more about it just now. (*Moving to door* R.) I must go.

STELLA. Only a few minutes ago I was happy. (*Returning to below chair above fire.*) I thought it couldn't last long. It didn't even last as long as I thought.

FARRANT. It didn't deserve to last a second. I'll get my coat.

(*He goes into room* R. STELLA *makes a great effort to avoid breaking down altogether. As* FARRANT *reappears with his cap and coat*, CHARLES *appears in the other doorway with a whisky and soda in his hand.*)

CHARLES. What? Going?

FARRANT (*curtly*). Yes. Good-bye.

(STELLA *turns away from them.* CHARLES *stands aside on* L. *of door to let* FARRANT *pass.* FARRANT *goes out at door up* C. *The outer door is heard to bang off.* STELLA *is still turned away.*)

CHARLES (*who has no malice in him, an insensitive, good-humoured chap*). I'm sorry, Stella. (*Coming to* L. *of her.*) Didn't mean to barge in at the wrong moment like that. Always putting my foot in it. No tact. It's just cost me a job. You'll laugh when I tell you about it.

(STELLA *stares straight in front of her. She is not sulking, but is temporarily oblivious of anything but her own misery.*)

Shall I tell you?

(STELLA *crosses to up* L. *and lights the lamp on piano.*)

Perhaps I'd better keep it. No good spoiling the story. But you will laugh when I tell you. (*He takes a good gulp of his whisky and soda, and looks across at her rather wistfully.*)

STELLA (*turning to him, in a muffled voice*). Why have you come here?

CHARLES (*trying to keep it light*). Oh—well—you see, I was resting and a bit fed up with town. Thought the change might do me good. All in order, you know. I had an invitation to come down here. I thought it might have come—indirectly—from you.

STELLA. It didn't.

CHARLES. No, I'm gathering that. Nobody seems to know much about me here. Haven't met your father yet.

STELLA. No—that's not going to be easy.

CHARLES. Why?

STELLA. I can't explain.

CHARLES (*sitting on left arm of chair, above fire*). I'm beginning to feel like a baby that's turned up at a wedding. A warm welcome was given to Mr. Charles Appleby, always a favourite in the North of England. Good old Charlie, they cried.

STELLA (*wearily*). Oh—don't be funny, Charlie.

CHARLES. Well, I've got to be something. Damn it, look at it from my point of view. I've got feelings as well as you and your old friend, the bronzed, clean-living English gentleman who's just pushed off in a temper. I come here because I'm invited. I imagine you've something to do with it. After all, you're still my wife.

(STELLA *sits on rocking-chair down* L.)

I get up at some unearthly hour this morning—in pitch darkness—travel most of the day, and then when I arrive here, I'm treated as if I were a bad dose of small-pox.

STELLA. Oh, I know. It's not your fault.

CHARLES. By the way, what's the telephone number here?

STELLA. I don't know. It's there.

(*He rises and goes over to telephone, and notes number on his cuff.*)

CHARLES. I must send it to the agents. They may want me in a hurry. (*Dropping down* C.) One or two new tours going out. Somebody said something about "Old Heidelberg" touring again.

(*There is a pause. He looks at her.*)

And "The Monk and the Woman." A title like that ought to bring 'em in. (*Going to* R. *of table.*) You know that Hilda Moore's touring in "Bella Donna." If she wants to get back to town and they want to keep the tour going, there might be a chance for you there—you've played Hilda Moore parts.

STELLA. I've finished with the theatre.

CHARLES. Don't believe it. (*Going to piano.*) I've heard that before. Nobody's finished with the theatre until the theatre's finished with them. You'll be working again in a month.

STELLA (*shaking her head*). I shan't.

CHARLES. I've said that, you know. We all have. Meant it too when we've said it. (*Leaning on piano.*) I remember once—it was about two years before I met you—I was out in "A Message From Mars"—and——

(*Enter* LILIAN *up* C., *carrying account books, etc. She goes to telephone-table for pen and ink and brings them to* R. *of table,* L.C.)

Hullo! You look business-like.

LILIAN. I have to do Dad's accounts.

STELLA (*with hostility*). Why? (*She rises.*)

LILIAN. He's so forgetful now.

STELLA. Oh. I haven't noticed it.

LILIAN. You haven't been here long enough to notice it.

CHARLES (*looking from one to the other*). Er . . . no. I think I'll have a look round.

(*He escapes at door up* C.)

(*Nothing is said for a moment.*)

STELLA (L. *of table*). It was you, of course, who asked Charles to come here.

LILIAN. Yes.

STELLA. How did you find him?

LILIAN. You'd told me his name and you said that you both had the same agent. When I was helping to turn out your room, I saw a letter from your agent——

STELLA. I see. Quite simple. These things usually are if you don't mind going into other people's rooms and reading their letters.

LILIAN. Perhaps if you'd condescended to do your own room—instead of going out for a walk with Geoffrey, I shouldn't have seen the letter.

STELLA. I wasn't asked to help with the housework here, was told, in fact, not to do anything. On the other hand, I *was* asked to go for a walk by Geoffrey. But that has nothing to do with it. You read my letter, probably read all my letters.

LILIAN. I've not the least desire to read your letters. That particular one happened to be lying open on your dressing-table. Your agent's name and address on it were big enough to be read a yard away.

STELLA. I'm glad he saved your eyesight. (*She turns away to window and then back again.*) Why did you ask Charles to come here? It was no business of yours. I'd told you that we had separated. We haven't lived together for over a year. We haven't spoken to one another, haven't seen one another—except the other day at the agent's—for months and months. If I'd wanted him here, I would have asked him myself. You'd no right to interfere. (*Pacing up and down* L. *of table.*) And if it had been anybody else but Charles—who's a fool he'd never have come here on such an invitation.

LILIAN. Three years ago, you were sufficiently in love with him to marry him. Now you can't stand him in the same house. (*She moves away towards fire with her back to* STELLA.)

STELLA. That's my affair.

LILIAN. By the way, I've put him in Wilfred's room.

STELLA. I suppose I ought to be grateful you haven't put him into my bed.

LILIAN. You needn't be disgusting.

STELLA. And you needn't be such a beastly little hypocrite. Why did you send for him?

LILIAN. He was your husband. You weren't happy, I could see that. I thought you'd like another chance.

STELLA. All lies. You're still talking like a beastly little hypocrite. You're lying, Lilian, you're lying. (*Going above table to* L. *of* LILIAN—*who is above pouf.*) *Why did you send for him?*

LILIAN. I've told you.

STELLA. You've told me nothing, and you know it. But I'll

make you tell the truth. (*Moving away to* c.) You made me confess about my marriage, you've read my letters, you've interfered in my private affairs—and now you imagine you can put me off with a few silly lies. (*Going nearer and to* L. *of* LILIAN *again.*) Do you think I'm a fool?
LILIAN (*contemptuously*). Yes.
(STELLA, *blazing with fury, slaps her face, hard. The effect is very marked on each.* LILIAN *stands rigid, filled with a cold anger.* STELLA *steps back and then turns away, trembling, her anger rapidly vanishing. She sits down at* R. *of table.*)
STELLA. I oughtn't to have done that. I'm sorry, Lilian.
LILIAN (*contemptuously*). It doesn't make me think you any less of a fool. It's like nearly everything else you do—violent and silly and useless.
STELLA (*rising—roused again*). Is it? Well, I'll tell you now why you sent for Charles. It had nothing to do with me and my marriage. You don't care a rap about that. Do you?
LILIAN (*calmly*). Not much. Why should I?
STELLA. No, you did it because you're in love with Geoffrey Farrant. What's the use of pretending? You know. And I know. You're in love with Geoffrey, and you're terrified of losing him. I knew that the very first night I came back, when you went sulking off to bed, pretending you'd a headache. Even before that, before Geoffrey called, the moment I arrived, I knew there was *something*. You didn't really want me back here. I felt at once there was something resentful about you.
LILIAN (*herself roused now, but still colder and harder than the other*). And why should there be anything else? (*She crosses to* R. *of* STELLA, *pressing her back against the table.*) Why should you expect us all to fall on your neck the minute you condescended to come home again?
STELLA. That's unfair——
LILIAN. It isn't. And if you didn't think about yourself all the time, you'd soon see that. You always had more of everything than Wilfred and I had. Before you went away, you let Geoffrey fall in love with you, made him follow you round, laughed at him —yes, and to us, and even then, I hated you for it——
STELLA. I cared more for Geoffrey then than you think.
LILIAN. I don't believe you know what it is to love anybody properly. You think being sentimental is caring for people. It isn't. (*She crosses above* STELLA *and above table to window.*) Then you insisted on going on the stage, although you knew very well that Mother had a horror of theatres. She couldn't help it. That's how she'd been brought up. You went away, without caring how much Mother and Father were worrying.
STELLA. That's not true. I cared terribly. You can't begin to understand——

D

LILIAN (*leaning over table, from* L. *of it*). That helped to kill Mother.

STELLA (*breaking down*). Oh—you're cruel, Lilian. That's not true. That's not true. (*She sits* R. *of table.*)

LILIAN. Yes, it is. You said you'd make me tell the truth, and here it is. Mother died. Father was left lonely and miserable. I didn't want to stay here all my life. I had plans of my own. But I had to stay then, to look after the house and Father. He needed me.

STELLA (*through her tears*). He didn't. (*Rising.*) If you'd decided to do something away from home he wouldn't have tried to stop you. He simply thought you wanted to stay at home.

LILIAN. How do you know?

STELLA. He—(*moving away to* c.) oh, it doesn't matter. The point is, you stayed at home because you wanted to stay at home. And now you're making a great virtue out of it. You're one of these self-appointed martyrs.

LILIAN. I'm not pretending to be a martyr. I'm simply explaining why I didn't think you were so very wonderful. You went off, not caring about us, to do what you wanted to do. And while you were enjoying yourself, you didn't bother about us. You could even get married without telling us. Then, when you thought you'd had enough of the stage and had made a mess of your marriage, you decided to come home.

STELLA. Yes, and you seem to forget that, after all, it's my home just as much as it's yours.

LILIAN. No, it isn't, and you know very well it isn't. It stopped being your home when you ran away from it, years ago. (*Crossing above table to fire.*) And it's my home, more than ever, because I've stuck to it and helped to keep it going. We'd made a life here without you, and now you have to come charging back into it, upsetting everyone.

STELLA (*going to* L. *of* LILIAN). Upsetting everyone? You seem to forget that everybody here was glad to see me again—except you.

LILIAN (*with her back to* STELLA). Yes, and a lot of good it'll do them.

STELLA. All you're thinking about is Geoffrey, Geoffrey, only you won't admit it.

LILIAN (*turning to her*). I'm not afraid of admitting it. I do love Geoffrey—I have done for years—and I believe I could make him happy. And I know you couldn't, and wouldn't even try very long.

STELLA. So you made up your mind at once that he must see for himself that I have a husband. . Oh—yes, they've met already. (*Going to table.*) I'm sorry you weren't here.

LILIAN. It wasn't just that. You have a life of your own—a life that you've made quite apart from us—you can't run away from it.

STELLA. But you see, I'm away from it now. And I'm not running back to it. You've done your best. Charles is here—and he's a nuisance—but he won't stay long. But I'm staying. You've played your trick, Lilian—and a very dirty little trick it was—but you haven't won. Nothing has happened except that now I realize that either you've changed completely or I never really knew you.

LILIAN. I can't see that it matters which it is.

(*Pause.* STELLA *crosses and sits on left arm of chair above fire.*)

STELLA (*distressed*). What does matter to me is that you and I could have talked to one another as we have done. I've never even tried to hurt you, and you've deliberately hurt me. I'd looked forward so much to seeing you again. We'd shared so many things before. I thought we'd be able to have a wonderful time together. If you'd been open and friendly from the first, I couldn't have taken anything, anybody, away from you. I could have been happy just because you were happy. Oh—Lilian—you wouldn't be so hard if you hadn't been shut up here so long in a safe little corner. It's because you don't know how much misery there is in the world, how circumstances and time can change and hurt us.

LILIAN. You're not really unhappy now. In a way you're enjoying it. You see, I'm not made like that. I can't enjoy my emotions.

(CHARLES *appears in doorway up* C.)

CHARLES (*to* STELLA). I say, Stella, your father's just come in. He thinks I'm a patient. You'd better come and explain.

(*He goes out.*)

STELLA (*rising, in a low voice*). I hope you don't think I'm going to enjoy this.

LILIAN (*scornfully*). You're not afraid of Dad, are you?

STELLA. I'm afraid for him. (*She moves away towards table.*) You can't begin to understand how hateful this is going to be for me. (*She goes to the door and calls, with assumed cheerfulness.*) Dad!

DR. KIRBY (*off*). Hallo.

STELLA. Just a minute.

DR. KIRBY. I'm in the surgery.

(STELLA *goes off at door up* C. LILIAN *sits down above and* R. *of table to her accounts and gradually loses control of herself. She is crying.*)

CURTAIN.

ACT III
SCENE 1

SCENE.—*As before.*

TIME.—*Late on Saturday night.*

When the CURTAIN *rises, the room is empty. The lamp on the piano is lit, but turned low. There is a good fire. On the table are a tray, holding a thermos flask, a decanter of brandy, a glass, some biscuits (in biscuit-jar) and another tray with whisky decanter and soda syphon and glasses on it. A clock outside in the hall strikes twelve. Before it has finished striking a door slams and the voices of* CHARLES *and* WILFRED *are heard outside.* CHARLES *enters first, looks round the room, goes to piano and begins turning up the lights. He is dressed as in Act II.* WILFRED *staggers in, with a folded mackintosh slung over one shoulder, and he sticks to this for some time. They are both drunk.* WILFRED *is the worse of the two. It should be quite obvious that they are drunk, but they must not indulge in the usual antics, and though their voices are thick, they must be clearly heard. There must be no hiccupping.*

CHARLES, *having turned up lamp on piano, goes down* L. *of table and crosses below it to fire, surveying room before he speaks.* WILFRED *goes to below piano.*

CHARLES (*looking round the room*). Nice. Very nice. I call this very snug, old boy.

WILFRED. Not bad qua'ers, not bad qua'ers at all. Wish I'd something like this in Bri'sh West.

CHARLES (*solemnly*). In where, old boy?

WILFRED (*solemnly*). Bri'sh West.

CHARLES. Never heard of it.

WILFRED (*deliberately*). Bri-tish West—Africa.

CHARLES. Oh—yes. Africa. I've been to Africa—South Africa. It's all right, Africa is, old boy.

WILFRED (*going to* L. *of and above* CHARLES, *trailing mackintosh on floor, very seriously*). It's fine. I like Africa, Charlie.

CHARLES. Quite right. We pass Africa. (*Going to table, to above it.*) Hello, drinks. But what's this business?

WILFRED (*to* R. *of him, peering at the thermos flask*). That's for my father.

CHARLES. Where is he?

WILFRED (*waving a hand*). Out—working. Somebody somewhere must be very ill. Having a baby p'r'aps. Or pegging out.
CHARLES. And your poor old governor's looking after 'em.
WILFRED. Yes, and that's for when he comes in. Hot milk. Brandy. Biscuits. And he deserves 'em, Charlie.
CHARLES. He does, old boy. He's a noble fellow. As soon as I saw him—yesterday afternoon—I said to myself : " Stella's father—my father-in-law—he's a noble old fellow." (*Picking up whisky decanter and smelling it.*) I think we ought to drink his health.
WILFRED (*solemnly*). I ag-agree. (*He goes above* CHARLES *and comes down* L. *of table to rocking-chair. He drops his mackintosh on chair, but it falls on the floor instead.*)

(CHARLES *pours out two whiskies and soda during the next two speeches. He first of all pours out a large one for himself, has a look at* WILFRED *and decides to pour him out a small one.*)

CHARLES (*with air of profundity*). If my old man had been a doctor, a lot of things would have been different—very different. But he wasn't.
WILFRED. What was he—your old man?
CHARLES (*very solemnly*). Nothing, old boy—nothing. Just a bloody English gentleman. (*Getting to* R. *of table.*) But never mind him. (*Sternly, raising glass.*) Here's to Dr. Kirby—a noble old fellow.
WILFRED (*raising glass*). Here's to him—good old Dad.
CHARLES (*suddenly sitting* R. *of table, before he speaks, still solemnly*). Let's sit down.
WILFRED. Yes. (*He sits* L. *of table.*)

(WILFRED *looks rather sleepy.*)

CHARLES. You know, old boy—we've had a good evening. I told you yesterday when we first met—I said then, " We can go out—you and I—and have a good evening here." Didn't I?
WILFRED. You did.
CHARLES. Well, we've had one. (*He starts to laugh and puts pipe in his mouth, upside down.*) What was the name of the fellow that gave us a lift in the trap?
WILFRED. Harper.
CHARLES. Harper. A very nice fellow—Harper. But he was badly screwed, y'know, old boy. He ought to have let me drive.
WILFRED. I met a fellow on the boat coming home called Harper. He came from Manchester and he had a glass eye. I hate glass eyes.
CHARLES (*filling his pipe*). And I hate Manchester. If I'd to choose between Manchester and a glass eye, I'd rather have a glass eye. You meant a glass eye, old boy, didn't you—and not an eyeglass?
WILFRED. Yes, glass eye. One of our chaps in the Company——

CHARLES. What company? You're not on the stage, you're in Africa.

WILFRED. Yes, I mean the Bri'sh West African Company. He has an eyeglass. He says he used to own two racehorses when he was home. Awful nut.

CHARLES. Probably lying, old boy. There's a terrible lot of lying about. When you're my age you'll have found that out. Everybody lies like the devil. Women worse than men.

WILFRED. That's true, Charlie. A girl on the boat told me a lot of lies. (*With sudden energy.*) Absolute lies.

CHARLES. I know, I know. If I'd had a sovereign for every lie that girls on boats have told me, I'd be rich man now. (*He strikes a match and throws it away over his shoulder, without lighting his pipe.*) And I'll tell you another thing about women, old boy. Women—and I don't care who they are—all women—can't stand seeing men enjoy themselves *by* themselves. It annoys 'em. It makes 'em furious. They like to think they're indis-indispensable. We've had a good evening, haven't we?

WILFRED. Yes.

CHARLES. All right then. We've had a good evening. No harm in it, no harm in it at all. A few pubs. A few rounds of drinks. A talk with some of the local boys. Social harmony and innocent mirth, as somebody said somewhere. A good evening. But do you think you could get any woman to admit we'd had a good evening? No, old boy. Take it from me. You couldn't. Stella's a nice girl. Would she admit we'd had a good evening? No. Your other sister —Lilian—would she admit it? No. Old boy, they'd turn it down flat. "Where have you been? Look at you." *All alike.* (*He strikes another match, this time lighting his pipe, and this match, likewise, goes over his shoulder.*)

WILFRED. Well, I don't know. There's a girl I could mention— lives round here—and I don't think she——

CHARLES (*holding up his hand*). She's different. (*Having felt for another match, he finds the box empty: so he rises, crosses to fire and gets another box from mantelpiece.*) Don't you believe it. They're all different—they don't mind anything—no, not until they've got hold of you. But once they've got you, they won't have this, they won't have that. The thing—the very thing—they told you once they liked you for—that's what they want you to change, old boy. If they liked your little jokes before you were married, then after you're married they ask you why you're always trying to be funny. See what I mean? (*He again strikes a match and throws it away.*)

WILFRED. Yes, I suppose so. One of our chaps in Africa——

CHARLES. Just a minute. Tell me afterwards. Don't forget. I want to hear about that chap. But what I was going to say was this. It doesn't matter what women do, or who tells you lies, or whether you go to Africa or not, life's a very wonderful thing. Do you realize that, old boy?

WILFRED. By Jove—yes. I was just thinking coming along——
CHARLES. A wonderful thing. You can't get away from that.
WILFRED. You can't get away from it, Charlie.
CHARLES (*crossing back to* R. *of table, stepping with difficulty over pouf*). I've had my troubles. Even you've had your troubles——
WILFRED. I should think I have. Do you know when I first went out to Nigeria——
CHARLES. You had a hell of a time. Yes, and I've had a hell of a time. But in spite of everything, I think—I *know*—life's a wonderful thing.
WILFRED. There's *something* about it, isn't there?
CHARLES. You've hit it. There's *something* about it. Here I am—in—where is it?
WILFRED. Where's what?
CHARLES. Here—this place.
WILFRED. Eden End.
CHARLES. Here I am in Eden End. Never been here before—may not ever come here again——
WILFRED. I hope you will, Charlie.
CHARLES. I hope so, too, old boy. But you never know. (*He sits* R. *of table.*) That's another thing about life (*very solemnly*)—you never know. A week ago I didn't know I was going to be here—sitting here with you.
WILFRED. And I didn't know you existed.
CHARLES. Didn't you? Dam' shame. (*He drinks.*) But there you are, you see. Here I am. And here you are. Having a drink together. Everything's quiet. Women asleep upstairs—(*turning to look at door up* C.) or I hope they are. Your governor out there somewhere—helping some poor devil out of the world—or perhaps helping some other poor devil into the world—and here we are. And you'll go back to Ceylon——
WILFRED. Africa.
CHARLES. It's all the same, old boy. This isn't geography. And I'll go back to town. Get a job. Go on tour again perhaps. People will come to see me. They don't know much about me. I don't know anything about them. Never mind. Perhaps I make 'em cry. Perhaps I make 'em laugh. And, mind you, old boy, give me a part with the ghost of a bit of comedy in it, and I *can* make 'em laugh. I can make 'em yell. Weedon Grossmith—Weedon Grossmith, mind you—once said to me: "You've got a touch, Appleby, old boy. You've *got* something." And I have. The trouble is—and this is where *luck* comes in—most of the time I've had to make something out of nothing.
WILFRED. I'll bet you're awfully good, Charlie. Do you know what old Stansted—one of the Company's chief men out there—said about me?
CHARLES. No? (*He attends to his pipe again.*)
WILFRED. He didn't say it *to* me, but he told one of the other

fellows. He said that of all the young men who'd come out lately I'd got the best idea of handling the natives.

CHARLES. I'm not surprised, old boy. It doesn't surprise me at all. That's because you've got sympathy. You're human. You're like me. You've either got it or you haven't got it. We've got it. (*He strikes a match, re-lights his pipe and again throws the match over his shoulder.*)

WILFRED (*sleepily*). We've got it. (*He yawns slightly.*) I think —you're an awfully fine chap, Charlie. And I'm glad you came to stay with us.

CHARLES. Thanks, old boy. So am I. All the best. (*Drains his glass.*)

WILFRED. All the best. (*Drains his and then drops the glass.*)

CHARLES (*getting up*). We'd better be getting upstairs. (*Going up to door* C.) What was the name of that biggish place at the cross-roads?

WILFRED. That's the "White Hart." My favourite.

CHARLES. Quite right. Best of the lot. We'll concentrate on that one next time. Did you notice the little barmaid there, the little fair one?

WILFRED. Yes. That's Alice.

CHARLES. Alice, is it? Well, she's all right. A promising little tart, that. (*He drops down* R.C. *and hums or sings* "*Where My Caravan has Rested.*")

WILFRED (*suddenly rigid with attention*). Why do you call her that?

CHARLES (*carelessly*). Didn't you notice her? Something doing there, old boy. Can't miss it. Quite pretty and absolutely asking for it. Didn't you see her giving me enormous glad eyes? Wanted me to come round and see her when it was quieter.

WILFRED (*suddenly shouting*). She didn't. (*He rises and goes below table to* L. *of* CHARLES: *jogging his arm.*) You're a liar.

CHARLES (*good-humouredly*). Here, steady, steady.

WILFRED (*not so loud now, but with intensity*). I tell you she didn't, and you're a dirty liar.

CHARLES. You're screwed, ole boy. Take it easy.

WILFRED (*half shouting, half crying*). Tell me it isn't true.

CHARLES. Anything you like so long as you stop making that row. What the devil does it matter whether it's true or not?

WILFRED. It matters to me.

CHARLES. Oh—I see.

WILFRED. It's the only thing that matters to me.

CHARLES. Don't be a damned fool. Of course it isn't.

WILFRED (*vehemently, clutching hold of the other*). She didn't ask you to come round and see her, did she? Tell me she didn't. (*Raising his voice.*)

CHARLES. Not so much noise, you young ass.

WILFRED. Tell me she didn't.

Sc. 1.]   EDEN END.

(CHARLES *puts* WILFRED *across in front of him and gets him into chair below fire.*)

CHARLES. She didn't, then. It must have been somebody else—one of the others.

WILFRED (*distressed*). Are you sure?

CHARLES. What I am sure of, old boy, is that you're badly screwed and that it's time I got you up to bed.

(LILIAN, *in night things and a dressing-gown, has opened the door* C. *and stands in the doorway*—L. *of door—looking at them.*)

LILIAN. You're making a frightful noise. (*She comes more into room.*)

CHARLES. Sorry—Lilian. Just been having a little argument, that's all. I'm taking Wilfred up to bed now. He's a bit—tired.

LILIAN (*contemptuously*). You mean he's drunk. You both are.

CHARLES (*indignantly*). Oh—no, no, no, no.

(STELLA, *also in night things and dressing-gown, appears in open doorway up* C.)

STELLA. What's the matter? (*She crosses to below* WILFRED *in chair below fire.*) Oh, Charles!

WILFRED (*miserably*). I think—I'm going—to be sick.

(CHARLES *and* STELLA *help* WILFRED *to his feet.* CHARLES *is on* R. *of* WILFRED *and has his left arm.*)

CHARLES (*putting arm round him*). That's all right, old boy. That's all right. You stick to me. Steady, steady. (*To* STELLA *and* LILIAN.) I'll look after him. (*To* WILFRED, *who is groaning.*) That's all right, old boy. I've got you. Steady, steady. (*To the girls.*) Don't worry. He's all right.

(*He escorts him through the doorway. He can be heard, repeating his* "All right" *and* "Steady" *outside.* STELLA *stands near the doorway, watching them.* LILIAN *still stands* L. *of door, watching* STELLA. *Finally the latter closes the door, and comes in, looking troubled.* STELLA *comes to above table.* LILIAN *comes down* L. *of table, picks up mackintosh, folds it and puts it on rocking-chair. She then picks up tumbler and puts it on table. Crosses below table to fire and resets pouf. She picks up the burnt matches.*)

LILIAN. Thank God, Dad's still out, that's all.

STELLA. That's what I was thinking.

LILIAN. He hates drunkenness. So do I.

STELLA. He needn't know anything about this.

LILIAN. Don't imagine that I shall tell him. But this has never happened before. Wilfred does go into the local pubs sometimes, but he's never had much to drink. As a matter of fact, I believe he thinks he's fallen in love with a barmaid somewhere. But he's never been like this before.

STELLA. No, this comes of going out with Charles—the very first night too.
LILIAN. And—I hope—the last.
STELLA. I didn't ask Charles to come here. He's your guest.
LILIAN. He's your husband.
STELLA. He was.
LILIAN. He still is. (*A pause.*) Why did you marry him, Stella?
STELLA. For the usual reasons. I was in love with him. Queer, no doubt—but true. (*Yawning.*) As a matter of fact I was very much in love with him.
LILIAN. Were you?
STELLA. Poor Charlie! I suppose it does seem incredible to you. I think I'll have one of Dad's biscuits. (*Takes one.*) You have one. (*She takes biscuit-jar to* LILIAN.)

(LILIAN *has one.*)

LILIAN. Has he changed very much?
STELLA (*returning with biscuit-jar to above table*). No, he hasn't—really. But it's one thing seeing him here, quite out of his element, not working, rather depressed. And it's quite another thing seeing him—as I did for months when we were touring the East and Australia—as the most amusing and charming person in the company. And to be working and travelling and laughing with him month after month, thousands of miles from home. It's no use, Lilian, you can't begin to understand my life. We were very happy for a time. Poor Charlie.
LILIAN (*sitting on club fender*). Why do you say " Poor Charlie "?
STELLA. Because—although he doesn't deserve it—(*crossing and sitting above* LILIAN *on club fender*) I can't help feeling sorry for him. I suppose I'm still fond of him.
LILIAN. Then why don't you look after him?
STELLA. Why should I?
LILIAN. He belongs to you.
STELLA. I can't think about people like that. I'm not possessive. (*Startled.*) What's that?

(*It is* CHARLES, *looking in at the door* C. *He is soberer than he was, but still ripe—and very sleepy.*)

CHARLES. Are you two quarrelling again? You're always quarrelling. Why don't you take it easy? Live and let live.
STELLA (*sharply*). Never mind about us. What about Wilfred?
CHARLES (*coming farther into room*). That's what I came down to say. He's been sick. He's in bed. He's fast asleep.
STELLA. Well, you get to bed now, Charles, and you can both sleep as long as you like in the morning.
CHARLES. It was his own fault, you know. He would mix them.

I said to him—right at the first, I said " Now, take my tip, and don't mix 'em." But he wouldn't——

STELLA (*rising*). Oh—get to bed, Charlie. And don't make a noise. Father may be in any minute.

CHARLES. A noble old fellow. Wouldn't disturb him for the world.

(*He goes to door, then turns back to girls and speaks in a whisper.*)

Good night, girls.

(*He goes out, tripping over step on his way.*)

STELLA. Poor Charlie. (*Going to above table.*) Nobody knows better than I do how maddening he can be, but there's something rather sweet about him. He's only a great child. There are dozens of them—great children, just like him—in the theatre.

LILIAN. Well, if he's a child, all the more reason why you should look after him.

STELLA (*taking another biscuit*). Don't nag at me, Lilian.

LILIAN (*sitting on floor in front of fire, leaning on pouf—back to fire facing* C.). And child or no child, he can't be allowed to spend any more evenings like this with Wilfred.

STELLA. Well, if Wilfred is developing a passion for barmaids, he's quite capable of getting drunk by himself.

LILIAN. No, he isn't. Wilfred's only a silly baby yet. Besides, it's Dad I'm really thinking about.

STELLA. Yes, there's Dad. (*She crosses and sits in armchair above fire.*)

(*Pause.*)

LILIAN. Well?

STELLA. You're just trying to drive me out, aren't you, Lilian? I can't understand you. You seem to have no feeling for me at all, less than a stranger would have. It doesn't seem to matter to you that I've been desperately unhappy these last months and that when I came home it was like beginning a wonderful new life. Doesn't that mean anything to you, Lilian?

LILIAN. Yes. And it would mean a lot more if I really believed in it.

STELLA. You think it's all insincere, made-up stuff, an actress letting herself go—don't you?

LILIAN. I think you encourage your emotions, so that whatever they are—in a way—you enjoy them.

STELLA. We shall never agree, of course. We've grown up to be thousands of miles away from each other. We live in different worlds. I think you're rather like Mother.

LILIAN. I think I am.

STELLA. But what hurts me is that, underneath all this difference, there isn't, with you, any affection or friendship. If you'd lived so long among strangers, in places where nobody knew or cared about you at all, you'd understand how this can hurt. You've behaved very badly to me—you've deliberately set yourself against me—and yet to me you're still Lilian, my sister, and I'm longing all the time to talk properly with you, to remember all the silly old things we did, to laugh and cry together. Can't you see?

LILIAN. The trouble is, Stella, you can afford to feel like that. I can't.

STELLA. What do you mean?

LILIAN. It hasn't been fun for me—treating you like this. It's not true that I don't care at all. I do. But I know—and I knew it the moment you came back—that if I gave in, you'd overwhelm me, sweep me away——

STELLA. And why not?

LILIAN. Because you'd knock down everything I've built up here. You'd take Geoffrey again, without really wanting him. You'd unsettle Dad, Wilfred, everybody and everything. And just when they'd all come to depend on you again, you'd run away—as you did before. People like you, Stella, don't want to make other people unhappy——

STELLA (*sitting forward*). I don't. Never, never. I know too much about it myself.

LILIAN. But, for all that, you *do* make people unhappy. You can't help it, I suppose. But there's no real responsibility in you.

STELLA (*in despair*). But why are you so responsible—so old and wise? You say I make people unhappy. I may do. I don't know. But I can make them happy too. Can you?

LILIAN. Yes, in my own way.

STELLA. And a dull and dusty way it seems, too.

LILIAN. No it isn't. What do you know about me?

STELLA. How can I know anything about you when you're all shut up inside yourself and won't come out? Oh—it's no use.

LILIAN. We'll never agree.

STELLA. I don't want us to agree. That doesn't matter. But we could at least be *real* together. Even that's impossible, it seems.

LILIAN. It's years too late. (*Rising.*) Let's be reasonable.

STELLA (*wearily*). Go on, then, let's be reasonable.

LILIAN. You saw what happened to-night? Wilfred—and your Charles. What are you going to do?

STELLA. I don't know. I want to think.

LILIAN. You'll go sooner or later, you know.

STELLA. Why should you say that? You don't know. You don't know what my life's been like. You don't realize what it's meant—coming back—home.

LILIAN. You'll soon get tired of it.

STELLA (*uncertainly*). No. No. I'm sure I shouldn't.

LILIAN (*mercilessly*). Just as you did before. You'd go on smashing things, other people's lives as well as your own. Dad thinks you've had a wonderful time on the stage——

(STELLA *rises*.)

—that you're going to be a famous actress, that you're happily married——

STELLA (*in distress*). I know. (*She crosses to piano and sits on piano-stool*.) Please, Lilian. I want to think.

LILIAN (*without malice, but forcefully*). If you wanted to stay, you'd have to tell him that you'd failed in everything. And that's only the beginning. You'd never get back into this life properly. You'd be restless. You'd be a person without a real life anywhere. You'd think yourself a failure.

STELLA (*stopping her*). Oh—stop, stop! I won't listen to any more.

(*The front door shuts rather noisily*.)

LILIAN. There's Dad coming in.

STELLA (*rising and going to* L. *of table*). You go to bed, Lilian. I want to talk to him for a minute.

LILIAN. Don't keep him up. He'll be awfully tired.

STELLA (*wearily*). No, no, I know. But I must talk to him. It may be for the last time.

(DR. KIRBY *enters* C. *He looks very tired*.)

DR. KIRBY. Mrs. Sugden's been delivered of a man-child so big and so like William Sugden that I felt like offering it a pipe of tobacco. (*He sits* R. *of table*.) Ah, well—I'm tired.

STELLA. You must be, Dad.

LILIAN. Your hot milk and brandy's here.

DR. KIRBY. Thanks.

(STELLA *pours out a glass of hot milk from thermos flask and sits* L. *of table*.)

But what are you two doing up?

STELLA. We both heard a noise. It was Charles, and Wilfred. They went to bed, but we stayed on, talking.

LILIAN (*crossing to him*). But I'm going now. (*She kisses his forehead*.) Good night.

DR. KIRBY.⎫
STELLA. ⎭Good night.

(LILIAN *goes out* C.)

(DR. KIRBY *puts some brandy in his milk*.)

DR. KIRBY. I'm getting a bit tired of the human body, Stella. I shall be glad to get back to my birds. I don't know that the behaviour of birds is much better than that of people. They can be as greedy and quarrelsome and vindictive as we can. But they're not so heavy and lumpy. They do things with more style. There's more enchantment about them. They ought to have had the fairy tales, not us.

STELLA. Perhaps they have their own. Was Mrs.—Sugden—difficult?

DR. KIRBY. Not really. (*He rises and pushes chair under table: he then takes his glass with him over to fire.*) Though it's always a worrying job, especially when you've had to wait overtime. But it's done now. And there's another of us arrived in the village.

STELLA. Poor little chap.

DR. KIRBY. Oh—you needn't be sorry for him. To begin with, he looks a fine healthy specimen—the Sugdens are. And then again, with any luck he'll see a better world than you and I will ever know. That's certainly true of me. (*He sits in chair above fire.*) I'm not one of these elderly men—and I meet enough of 'em—who think everything's going to the dogs.

(STELLA *rises, crosses above table and sits on floor by left arm of chair, above fire.*)

There's a better world coming, Stella—cleaner, saner, happier. We've only to turn a corner—and it's there. I don't suppose I shall turn it, but you will. And this baby of Sugden's won't know anything else. When he grows up—sometime in the Nineteen Thirties—he simply won't understand the muddle we lived in.

STELLA. It is a muddle, isn't it?

DR. KIRBY (*sipping his drink*). Yes, and it's mostly our own fault. Yet it isn't either. (*He puts his glass on club fender.*) Have you noticed—or are you too young yet—how one part of us doesn't seem to be responsible for our own character and simply suffers because we have that character? You see yourself *being* yourself, behaving in the old familiar way, and though you may pay and suffer, the real you, the one that watches, doesn't seem to be responsible.

STELLA (*eagerly*). Yes, I was thinking about that only to-night. It's true.

DR. KIRBY (*tenderly*). Queer to see you looking like that again, with your hair down. It makes the last twenty years seem like nothing. You might be a child again. (*He puts a hand on her hair, in an awkward caress.*)

STELLA (*gently*). Dad, I'm afraid Charles and I must go to-morrow.

DR. KIRBY. That's bad news, my dear. I'd hoped you were staying a long time.

STELLA. So had I. But—well—we've just been offered two very good parts.

DR. KIRBY. And you're right to take them. Though I think you could do with a longer holiday than you've had. But if the English Theatre won't even let go of you for a few weeks, we must put up with it, that's all.

STELLA. I don't want to go.

DR. KIRBY. You mustn't mind us. I'm proud of you. I like to think of you forging ahead in your profession, getting all you can out of life. You know, you're doing it for me, as well as for yourself. As I told you before, I think I made a mistake. Your mother wanted me to settle down here, so I did. Nobody knows but you that I've ever regretted it. That's our secret.

STELLA (*distressed, deeply affectionate, pressing her face against his arm*). Dad!

DR. KIRBY. You're rectifying that mistake, my dear. And only you. Lilian's your mother over again. As long as she's a house of her own—and a man in it—she'll be happy in her own way. Wilfred's a good lad, but he's a bit weak and easy-going. He'll never do much. (*Putting his left arm on her left shoulder.*) But you're going on, living as I could have lived. I'm glad. I'm proud. (*Feeling a tear drop on to his hand he turns her face to him.*) So there can't be anything to cry about.

STELLA (*jumping up*). Of course not. I'm stupid. And it's bedtime. (*She goes up to door* C.)

DR. KIRBY (*briskly*). Sunday to-morrow. Only one train to London. The four-twenty. And a brute.

STELLA. That's nothing. We're used to brutal Sunday trains. They're almost the only kind we know. (*Turning at door, trying to smile at him.*) Good night, Dad.

DR. KIRBY. Good night, Stella. (*He sips his milk and brandy.*)

CURTAIN.

SCENE 2

SCENE.—*Same as before.*

TIME.—*Sunday afternoon.*

It is a dark afternoon. The door C. *is open.* DR. KIRBY *enters, followed closely by* SARAH, *who is talking volubly and dividing her attention between the window and him.* SARAH *has brought in* STELLA'S *hat, muff and fur, which she places on table. She then goes to window.* DR. KIRBY *is trying as best he can to search through the drawers at the table. He looks in drawer* R. *of table, drawer below table and drawer* L. *of table, leaving the last open.*

SARAH. If you'd a bit o' sense you wouldn't let her stir out to-day, let alone go to London. Sunday an' all. Travelling o' Sunday in a fog. Nowt good'll come of that. It's as thick as ever it wor. Nay, thicker. It'll be worse afore it's better. What they want to run trains at all for o' Sundays, I don't know. Why can't they let folks have a bit o' peace and quiet for one day in the week?

(*Taking advantage of her back being turned,* DR. KIRBY *escapes* C. SARAH *does not notice or turn round.*)

Stop at home and sit by the fire. London 'ull still be there tomorrow.

(WILFRED *comes in* C.)

It'll keep, London will. Unless it goes rotten. Daft, I call it.
WILFRED. I say, Sarah. Who do you think you're talking to?
(*He looks in drawer of telephone table.*)
SARAH (*shutting drawer which* DR. KIRBY *left open*). Not to you.
WILFRED. Well, you're not talking to anybody else, because there's nobody else here. (*Looks in bookcase below fire.*)
SARAH. Then I'm wasting my breath.
WILFRED. The car'll be here in another quarter of an hour. (*He starts looking in drawer* R. *of table.*)
SARAH. Are they having a motor-car to take 'em to the station?
WILFRED. Yes, old Thompson's Arrol-Johnston.
SARAH. I call it tempting providence.
WILFRED. I can't find my records. Have you seen them?
SARAH. Do you mean the things for that talking machine?
WILFRED. Yes. I can't find them anywhere.
SARAH. I'll go and help Miss Stella to finish her packing. (*Moves towards door* C.)
WILFRED (*stopping her*—R. *of her*—*by door*). I believe you know where they are.
SARAH. You shall have 'em in the morning.
WILFRED. I thought as much. Cheek! Where've you put them?
SARAH. Where you won't find them.

(WILFRED *crosses below her to window, to look in window-seat.*)

We don't want no talking machines on a Sunday. You can play it to-morrow all day if you like.
WILFRED (*shouting*). I don't want to play it all day to-morrow. I want those records now. (*He shuts lid of window-seat with a bang.*)
SARAH. If I gave 'em you, you wouldn't have time to play 'em.

(DR. KIRBY *bustles in* C. *He goes to bookcase* R. *He is in a very fussy mood.* SARAH *darts at him.*)

(*To* L. *of* DR. KIRBY.) What you're letting Miss Stella go for to-day, Sunday, and wi' this fog and in a motor-car too, I don't know.

(SARAH *turns up and goes out* C.)

DR. KIRBY (*very fussily*). Don't be fussy, Sarah. Don't be fussy. I left a little book somewhere round here this morning.

(*There is a ring at the door.*)

(*Calling through open door* C.) See who that is, Sarah. (*Almost to himself.*) And I hope to goodness, I'm not going to be called away now.

SARAH (*calling off*). It's Captain Farrant.

DR. KIRBY (*calling to her and crossing above table, below* WILFRED, *to look in window-seat*). All right then, send him in, send him in. (*To* WILFRED.) It's a little book—about that size—called "Moorland Bird Life." Have you seen it?

WILFRED. No. (*Crossing to fire.*) And Sarah's hidden my gramophone records away somewhere, because it's Sunday. Damned cheek!

(FARRANT *appears in doorway up* C.)

DR. KIRBY. Hello, Geoffrey. Come into the surgery with me, will you? I want to get something for Stella to take away with her.

(DR. KIRBY *bustles him out up* C. WILFRED, *muttering* "Too much fuss," *lights a cigarette.* CHARLES *enters up* C.)

CHARLES. How's the head now?

WILFRED. Getting better, thanks.

CHARLES. You mixed 'em too much, old boy. (*Comes in and looks out of window.*) God!—what a beast of a day.

WILFRED (*not without gloomy satisfaction*). You'll have a rotten journey.

CHARLES (L. *of table*). I know we shall. You can't tell me anything about long train journeys on foggy Sundays. If we'd any sense, we'd stay here and sit in front of the fire and talk about West Africa and wild birds and operations and Gaby Deslys and the Bunny-Hug.

WILFRED. Can you do the Bunny-Hug?

CHARLES. No. Nor the Turkey Trot. Nor the Tango. Not my line—thank God! At the moment, I feel that my line is playing old family solicitors, rheumaticky, toothless old scoundrels. (*Imitates one.*) "I have been instructed, Sir Rupert, to acquaint you with the te-r-r-rms of your uncle's will."

WILFRED (*laughs*). Jolly fine; I wish I was an actor. (*He sits on chair below fire.*)

CHARLES (*gloomily*). And I wish I was in West Africa—the hottest and blackest bit. (*Coming above table to* L. *of him, lowering voice.*) By the way, just let me give you a tip, while I've a chance, old boy. Take it or leave it. But I think if I were you, I should give that pub—you know the one—the "White Hart"—a miss, and give the little girl Alice a miss with it. (*Going to fire.*) I don't want to interfere, old boy—and couldn't preach if I tried. But they're no good, those bits. Not to a youngster like you. She'll only lead you up and down the garden. I know. I've had some in my time. Give it a miss, old boy.

WILFRED (*sullen*). Yes—but you don't understand——

E

CHARLES. Absolutely understand everything. I've been there. I've had some. Just think it over, old boy.

WILFRED (*wearily*). The trouble is—— I'm having a hell of a time.

CHARLES (*patting him on the shoulder*). It'll pass. I know. Try and find another little girl. There must be plenty round here. Squires' daughters with round red cheeks who'll sing the Indian Love Lyrics to you after dinner. (*Sings, in burlesque manner,* " Ler-hess than the der-hust, Be-neath thy chariot whee-heel.")

(STELLA *enters* C. *dressed as in Act I. She comes to above table carrying a small case, which she puts on the table.*)

STELLA. Oh, Wilfred, Lilian wants you.

WILFRED (*gloomily*). All right.

(*He goes off* C., *shutting door.*)

CHARLES (*going* L. *of table*). Haven't you finished packing yet, old girl ?

STELLA (*coming down* L. *of table*). Very nearly. (*She picks up a book from rocking-chair down* L., *puts it on table and crosses below table to get another book from bookcase* R.) All but a couple of books. Charles, I want to talk to you.

CHARLES. And I want to talk to you. Haven't had a chance yet to-day. Look here, what's happening ? I get up——

STELLA (*crossing back to above table, to put books in bag*). At lunch time.

CHARLES. Admitted. And not feeling very bright. And I find we're leaving this afternoon. I gather, from what your father said, that we're supposed to have just been offered two wonderful parts.

STELLA (*hastily*). That's what I told him. I hope you didn't——

CHARLES. Now, now. You know me better than that. I murmured something about Tree and His Majesty's Theatre—big new production. Nearly convinced myself.

STELLA (*relieved*). That's all right, then.

CHARLES. Yes, as far as it goes. But I want to know what's happening.

STELLA (*crossing to* L. *of him, smiling faintly*). Well, we're both getting on the same train for town and sitting in the same compartment. Once we're out of sight, if you don't want to talk to me, you needn't, Charles.

CHARLES. I see. We're putting on a performance for these people here.

STELLA. Yes. It's probably the only performance we shall put on for some time, so we'd better make the best of it. (*She goes back to above table.*)

(*Pause.*)

CHARLES. Look here, Stella, couldn't we go on with it when we get to town ?

STELLA. Do you want to?
CHARLES. I do. You ought to know that. But do you, that's the point?
STELLA (*gravely*). I think I'd like to try again, Charles.
CHARLES (*happily*). That's wonderful of you, it really is, old girl.
STELLA (*half laughing, but sharp*). And don't call me " old girl."
CHARLES. Sorry, I forgot.
STELLA. How much money have you?
CHARLES (*humorously*). Now I know we *have* joined up again. Quite like old times. Yes, I've some money. About seventeen pounds. (*Going to* R. *of her.*) And then there's a fellow at the club who owes me a tenner——
STELLA (*speaking with him*). Who owes you a tenner—— He still doesn't count. You haven't much, have you? And I've only about twenty left. We shall have to get a job quick, Charles.
CHARLES. We'll walk into one to-morrow, now that we're together again. Might pick up a couple of leads for the road. What about trying for one of God's own countries again, eh?
STELLA. Yes, I wouldn't mind. In fact, I'd like it. If I'm going away, I might as well go a long way.
CHARLES (*moving away* R. *and sitting on left arm of chair above fire*). You're right, y'know, to clear out. You'd never settle here. All right for a break, but that's all. You're doing the right thing.
STELLA (*indulgently*). And am I doing the right thing—taking you back again?
CHARLES. It's a risk, I know—I'm no catch—but I won't let you down. We've had some fun together. We'll have some more yet. What do you say?
STELLA (*after a pause*). You've got the wrong tie on. (*She crosses to* L. *of him.*) Why do you keep wearing that tie?
CHARLES. It's the only one I brought. What's the matter with it?
STELLA (*patting his cheek*). It's awful.

(FARRANT *opens the door up* C.)

FARRANT. Oh—sorry.
CHARLES. That's all right. Come in, old boy. We're just having a chat about ties.

(FARRANT *comes in to* L. *of door.*)

STELLA (*going to above table*). We haven't long now. (*To* CHARLES.) Will you and Wilfred get my trunk down?
CHARLES (*rising and taking her case from table*). All baggage will be stacked in the hall—immediately.

(*He goes out* C. *whistling.* FARRANT *goes to fire.*)

STELLA. Well—Geoffrey?
FARRANT. You're going.

E*

STELLA. Very soon. Back to town.
FARRANT. I'm going too.
STELLA. You're going? Where? When?
FARRANT. I'm going out to New Zealand for a year or two, perhaps longer. To my cousin.
STELLA. But, Geoffrey, you were saying, only the other day, that you were so fond of this place you couldn't bear to leave it.
FARRANT. So I thought. Then I found I was wrong. I wanted to get away.
STELLA. And you've really made your mind up?
FARRANT. Yes. I cabled my cousin yesterday. I shall take the next boat.
STELLA (*involuntarily*). Poor Lilian!
FARRANT. Why do you say that?
STELLA. Don't you realize that Lilian's in love with you, and has been for years?
FARRANT (*embarrassed*). I'm sorry. Matter of fact, I'm very fond of Lilian. We've seen a lot of one another.
STELLA (*softly*). Then why don't you marry her, Geoffrey?
FARRANT. Because I don't want to, Stella. And I don't understand why you should ask me to. I don't understand women at all, I'm afraid. I can't make you out—for instance.
STELLA. Then don't try.
FARRANT (*crossing to* R. *of her*). I was angry with you when I left the other afternoon.
STELLA. I know you were, my dear. I'm sorry.
FARRANT. In a way, I'm still angry. But it's no use.
STELLA. It isn't any use being angry with people—like that. I'm beginning to see that.
FARRANT. I don't mean that—quite. I mean—well, here I am, you see. And I didn't know you were going when I called. I just couldn't keep away.
STELLA. But you were determined to go yourself—and a long way, too?
FARRANT. That was your doing, of course. I knew you'd be leaving us soon, and I felt you'd just leave me and the whole place as flat as a pancake. I couldn't stand the thought of that. I had to do something.
STELLA (*distressed*). I'm sorry. It's all such a muddle, Geoffrey, and I seem to be muddle-maker in chief. (*She comes down* L. *of and below table to* C.) For years, while I stayed away, I had the thought of this place—home—always in my mind, and here, I felt, it was different—no muddle. For an hour—no, only for half an hour—it was all I had thought it was, and I was so happy. Then I found it was all mixed up with the rest of the world. And now I haven't even got this to think about. (*She goes up to* R. *of him*.)
FARRANT. You talk too much about happiness, Stella.
STELLA (*with a faint smile*). I think I do, Geoffrey. I must be

a braver traveller. We have our lives to get on with, to live them as best we can. There's no running away. No escape. No miracles.

CHARLES (*off*). I'll give you a hand with those.

FARRANT. The others are coming. Good-bye, Stella. (*He takes her hand.*)

STELLA (*quickly*). But you're coming to the station?

FARRANT (*very quietly*). Yes, but this is the real good-bye. And good luck. I shall always love you.

STELLA. It's more than I deserve.

(*There is a noise of a car arriving.*)

Good-bye, my dear.

(*She kisses him, lightly, quickly. He crosses to* L. *of table. Stella drops down* C. *and crosses below table to* L. *Enter* CHARLES *carrying a tray on which are cups of tea, followed by* SARAH. *The car can be heard stopping outside.* DR. KIRBY *follows* SARAH *in. They are all wearing or carrying overcoats, etc., and are ready for the journey.* DR. KIRBY *puts his hat on piano. They take up the following positions.* CHARLES *is at the head of the table by tray,* FARRANT *on his* L. *and* DR. KIRBY *on his* R. STELLA *is down* L. *of table and* SARAH *down* R. *of it.*)

CHARLES. Enter ye butler! (*He puts tray on upstage end of table.*)

SARAH. I don't care if all the motor-cars in England is blowing and puffing and tooting outside, you're all going to have a good hot cup o' tea afore you go.

STELLA. Of course we are. Lovely tea. Thank you, Sarah. (*She crosses with cup of tea to chair below fire and sits.*)

(WILFRED *comes in up* C.)

WILFRED (*entering*). The car's here. (*At door.*) You haven't much time. (*He comes to top of table.*)

(DR. KIRBY *has drifted over to fire and* CHARLES *gets to down* R. *of him.*)

SARAH (*going off* R., *grumbling*). Plenty o' time. Let the thing wait.

(WILFRED *goes to window.*)

CHARLES (*trying tea, in low voice*). Strong stuff, isn't it?

DR. KIRBY (*also in low voice*). Far too strong. But she's made it specially. Must try and drink some just to please her.

CHARLES. Rather.

STELLA. Of course. (*In loud ringing tone.*) Lovely tea.

(LILIAN *comes in up* C. *and comes to top of table.*)

LILIAN. Hello, Geoffrey!

FARRANT (L. *of table*). Hello, Lilian!

LILIAN (*smiling charmingly*). Isn't it a horrible day?
FARRANT. Beastly.
LILIAN. How's the roan?
FARRANT. Better than I thought. The vet says it's a sprain. (*He moves away negligently to window.*) What's the fog like now, Wilfred? (*He goes below* WILFRED *and joins him at window, looking out.*)

(*Enter* SARAH *from* R., *carrying small parcel. She goes to* L. *of* STELLA.)

SARAH. I'd nearly forgotten this, Miss Stella.
STELLA. What is it, darling?
SARAH. Why, your fancy dress I found the other day—very day you came home.
WILFRED. She doesn't want it, Sarah.
STELLA. Of course I do. I shall hang it up in my dressing-room—always, wherever I am. A lovely present, Sarah. And the tea's so good.
CHARLES. Extraordinary. (*He crosses and puts cup down on downstage end of table, passes below it and continues up* L. *to up* C.)
DR. KIRBY. Now, Sarah, you must stop in, y'know. No station for you. (*He goes to* R. *of table and puts his cup down.*)
STELLA. Good gracious, no! Much too cold and foggy for you. Besides, I can say good-bye to you much better here.
SARAH. All right, then. Won't you have a drop more tea, love?
STELLA. No, thank you, darling.
WILFRED. Time we were off. (*He goes up to door* C.)

(*There is a vague stir but no definite move towards the door.*)

CHARLES (*idly*). If that telephone rings when we've gone, I'll bet it's to offer me the biggest part I've ever known—and I'll miss it. (*He is putting his coat on and is* R. *of door, below telephone table.*)
WILFRED. More likely to ask me to go shooting rabbits with the Mowbrays.
DR. KIRBY (*picking up hat from piano and coming* C., *heartily*). Don't you worry. I'll be the person who'll be wanted. And I've a good idea who'll be wanting me—poor soul. Well, all ready?

(*They straggle out, first* WILFRED *and* DR. KIRBY, *then* LILIAN *and* FARRANT.)

CHARLES (*going down to* R. *of* SARAH, *with* STELLA'S *parcel*). Now, Sarah, old girl, you stay here and keep warm. And I'm delighted to have met you. Heard a lot about you from Stella, y'know. Good-bye. (*Holds out his hand.*)
SARAH. Good-bye. (*She shakes hands timidly.*)

(CHARLES *goes up to door.*)

And—look after her.

CHARLES (*turning at door with mock salute of sword*). With my life! Good-bye.

(*He goes out.*)

(WILFRED *picks up two bags in hall.* FARRANT *picks up* LILIAN's *mackintosh :* LILIAN *picks up her hat from chest.*)

SARAH. He's not a bad sort for an actor chap, though I'll bet he takes a bit o' watching. But you look after him, too, love. He's nowt but a big daft lad—like 'em all.

STELLA (*whispering*). Oh, Sarah. I don't know what to say. There aren't any words.

SARAH. Nay, love. Nay, little love. (*Adjusting* STELLA's *fur.*) And don't catch cold when you're coming out o' the theatres. (*Very softly.*) I'm an old woman now, a'most past my time. Happen I shan't see you again.

STELLA (*crying*). Yes, you will. You must.

SARAH. Oh, I'll see you sometime. There's a better place than this, love.

(*There is the noise of car engine starting up outside.*)

CHARLES (*off, calling*). Come on, Stella.

STELLA (*breaking loose*). I must go. Good-bye, Sarah, darling. (*She kisses* SARAH *and crosses below her to door up* C., *but returns to kiss her again : she then takes a last look round.*) Good-bye—everything.

(*She runs out blindly. The door bangs to behind her. Then the outer door is heard closing with a bang. There is the noise of the car going away.* SARAH *goes to the window, stares out for a moment, then closes the curtains, so that there is no light but that from the fire. She goes over to the fire and lights a taper. The telephone bell begins ringing.* SARAH *goes to the telephone with the lighted taper in her hand, holds the light close to it for a second, staring at it in bewilderment, then slowly withdraws into her own room* R. *The telephone ringing is fainter, the firelight fades, until at last there is silence and complete Black Out.*)

CURTAIN.

PROPERTY PLOT

Upright piano—Victorian, mahogany—tuned to pitch of orchestra.
Round table—mahogany, centre pillar—diameter, 3 feet 3 inches.
Square table—mahogany, centre pillar—2 feet square.
Revolving bookcase—mahogany—1 foot 6 inches square.
Occasional table—mahogany—kidney shape, 2 feet.
Shelves—3 mahogany—2 feet wide—fixed to wall.
Club fender—brass, upholstered brown leather.
Armchair—upholstered dark red leather—worn.
Easy chair—no arms, covered rose.
Pouf—low, square.
Rocking-chair.
Piano-stool—revolving.
2 single chairs—mahogany, Trafalgar, slat back—upholstered green
Music-rack—mahogany.
Standard lamp (oil).
Chest (in hall).
Grandfather clock (in hall).
Carpet—over all—Oriental velvet, terra, blue, red, etc., pattern.
Strip down steps. Blue pattern in hall.
Rugs—black sheepskin, at fire, window and doors.
Curtains—cream net, half-way up window.
Dark rose velour over window recess—brass rod and rings.
Pictures above door R.—gilt-framed oil Landscape.
    Between door R. and fire—gilt-framed oil Portrait of old man.
    Below it—1 group—Cricket Club.
        1 group—Football Club.
    Above fireplace—gilt-framed oil Pastoral.
    Around shelves—back wall—above—Engraving.
        R. of shelves—1 group—Girls' School.
        1 group—Football Club.
        L. of shelves—2 groups—Amateur Theatricals.
    Below shelves—1 group—Boys' School.
    Above table (square)—Calendar—Shakespeare Quotations.
    L. of door up C.—Print of Coblenz.
    Oval gilt frame (below above print).
    Between window and corner—Print.
    Below window—2 prints—one below the other.
    In hall—3 small water-colours, 1 R. of and 2 L. of clock.

ACT I

On Piano (from up to down stage).
    Vase with chrysanthemums.
    2-fold gilt portrait frames.
    Pile of music, with "The Pink Lady" waltz on top.
    Eastern ornament.
    Oil lamp.
    Ashtray and matches.
    Keyboard open; music-rest down.

On table L.C.
> Small square table-mat—in dark rose velour.
> Ashtray and matches.
> "Sketch" and "Illustrated London News."
> Pack of playing-cards.
> Book.

On table up C.
> Telephone (pattern 1912).
> Small stationery cabinet.
> Folding blotter.
> Glass inkpot.
> Brass pen-tray, with pen.

On bookcase (above door R.).
> Books.
> Ginger-jar.
> Silver portrait frame.
> Small portrait frame.
> Small vase.
> Work-basket—containing:
>> 3 pairs socks (pair on top with hole), darning-needle threaded with wool, thimble.

On table down L.
> Small nest of drawers, in mahogany.
> Tiny ornament.

On shelves up C.
> Top—2 china ornaments with mounted photo between them.
> 1st—Lacquer cigarette-box and three books.
> 2nd—Complete set of books.
> 3rd—Silver vase, silver trophy, silver christening mug.

Fireplace.
> Brass fire-irons.
> Brass helmet-shaped coal-scuttle, filled with coal.
> Small poker.

Upstage of fireplace (on wall).
> Brass toasting-fork.
> Brass pipe-rack with 3 pipes.
> Monk's-head ornament.

Downstage of fireplace (on wall).
> Container with thick tapers for spills.

On mantelpiece (from up to down stage).
> Vase with letters poked behind it.
> Ashtray and matches.
> Silver post card frame.
> Old-fashioned china figure.
> China castle.
> Old-fashioned china figure, "Llewellyn riding his goat."
> Small vase.
> Glass vase.
> Mounted picture.

Behind fire.
> Coach candle—to be lit after lights come up, throughout the play, and put out at end, immediately SARAH has lit taper, before final Black Out.

On club fender.
> Ashtray—on upstage corner.

On easy chair (below fire).
> Book, covered with brown paper—open face downwards.

On rocking-chair, down L.
> "Tatler."

On chest in hall.
  Blue and white ginger-jar, with autumn leaves.
  Brass tray with visiting-cards.
Music-rack, below piano.
  Filled with sheet music.
On window-seat L.
  Horn gramophone—set down stage, the horn projecting on stage.
  Record—" Everybody's doing it."
  Needle.
  Gramophone is not fully wound.
In box of window-seat.
  Tennis racket and golf-clubs on top.
Off-stage R.
  Pile of clean washing, for SARAH.
  R. *of door* C.
  Washing-basket, filled with old clothes and with STELLA'S fancy dress, for SARAH.
Effects.
  Door-slam.
  Door-bell—old-fashioned type.
Hand Props.
  WILFRED—small packet of Gold Flake cigarettes.

ACT II

Piano—Shut.
  Match ready in match-box, downstage corner.
  Table L.C.—*Strike* book, " Illustrated London News " and cards.
  Set " Punch," downstage R., and small bowl nasturtiums.
Table up C.—*Set* ginger-jar with marigolds.
        Pen ready.
Bookcase down R.—*Strike* ginger-jar.
  Set vase of heather.
        Brown-paper cover book—on top of others in shelf.
Club fender—" Yorkshire Post " on downstage corner.
Pouf—*Strike* work-basket.
Rocking-chair down L.—*Strike* " Tatler."
  Set chair another foot on to stage.
Chairs at table—*Re-set* as in Act I.
Window—*Strike* gramophone.
Off stage, R. *of door* C.—Glass containing whisky and soda for CHARLES.
  Account books, for LILIAN.
Effects.
  Wind machine.
  Rain effect.
Hand Props.
  FARRANT—Cigarettes in case, pipe.
  WILFRED—Pocket-book, trouser-clips.
  DR. KIRBY—2 letters.
  SARAH—Note.
  Mackintoshes for STELLA and FARRANT, glycerined to look wet.
  CHARLES—Pencil.

ACT III
SCENE 1

Piano—*Strike* pile of sheet music.
Table L.C.—*Strike* " Punch," " Sketch," matches and flowers.
  Set up stage R.—small square Japanese tray with thermos flask (hot milk), decanter with brandy, tumbler, biscuit-jar (biscuits).
        Up stage L.—black wooden tray with sparklet soda syphon, decanter of whisky and 2 tumblers.

Easy chair below fire.—*Strike* " Yorkshire Post."
Pouf—*Set* 1 foot up stage and nearer fire.
Chairs at table—*Set* down stage L. of table and up stage R. of table, the latter 1 foot away from table.
Rocking-chair down L. *Re-set* as in Act I.
Fireplace—Matches ready on mantelpiece.
Window—Curtains closed.
Effects.
  Clock-strike.
Hand Props.
  CHARLES—Pipe, tobacco pouch, matches.
  WILFRED—Mackintosh (carried).

SCENE 2
(Half-minute change.)

Table L.C.—*Strike* trays with glasses, etc.
Rocking-chair—*Set* small book.
Chairs at table—*Set* in to table and to enable all drawers to open.
Window—Curtains open.
Off stage, R.
  Brown-paper parcel for SARAH.
  R. *of door* C.
  Black wooden tray with 6 cups of tea, for CHARLES.
  Small black travelling bag, for STELLA.
  Gladstone bag and kitbag with Australian and Eastern labels.
  LILIAN'S mackintosh and hat (to put on chest).
  STELLA'S hat, muff and fur, for SARAH'S entrance.
Effects.
  Motor-car noise.
Hand Props.
  WILFRED—Cigarette.

www.ingramcontent.com/pod-product-compliance
Ingram Content Group UK Ltd.
Pitfield, Milton Keynes, MK11 3LW, UK
UKHW021846210426
5322IPUK00022B/495